Trimmers, Trucklers & Temporizers

Notes of MURAT HALSTEAD from the
Political Conventions of 1856

‡ ‡ ‡

Edited by
WILLIAM B. HESSELTINE
REX G. FISHER

THE STATE HISTORICAL SOCIETY OF WISCONSIN
MADISON 1961

Composed by Graphco, Inc., Neenah, Wisconsin
Printed by Cushing-Malloy, Inc., Ann Arbor, Michigan

Contents

‡   ‡   ‡

Introduction

‡   ‡   ‡

MURAT HALSTEAD, young Cincinnati journalist with an intense devotion to the principles of freedom and abolitionism, viewed the approach of the political campaign of 1856 with doubt and skepticism. On the eve of the meetings of the great party conventions, he feared, indeed, that the assembling politicians would slink away from the "great question" before the American People. The question was—and Halstead had no doubts about it—"SHALL SLAVERY BE EXTENDED?" Circumstances "beyond human control," he fervently asserted, "have fixed the political issue now before the people" and every honest man, honorable politician, and true republican desired to see a fair test of the question. But, he sadly noted, there were few honest men among the politicians, few who trusted the "ability of the masses for self-government," few who dared "to present an important issue in a direct form for political agitation and settlement." Instead, concerned only with party success and the emoluments of office, the politicians were trying to avoid the issue. They were searching for candidates who would offend nobody. They were seeking for coalitions which would submerge principle to expediency. They were "trucklers, temporizers and compromisers."[1]

In the fullness of time, Murat Halstead would become one of America's most distinguished political commentators, a journalist whose judgments on the behavior of politicians would be received with respect, and whose incisive comments would reveal to his readers the hidden processes by which the practitioners of the art of politics worked their shoddy miracles. In 1860 he would survey the splintering Democratic Party, bent on suicidal self-destruction at Charleston and Baltimore, and he would view with wonderment, if not with rapture, the Republican convention in Chicago's Wigwam which brought forth Abraham Lincoln as the party's candidate. His reports, published as *Caucuses of 1860*[2] would remain a basic source book for the conventions and a joy to future generations of historians who sought for insights on the political revolution which presaged the Civil War. From 1856 to his death in 1908, Halstead attended political conventions and reported them, first for the Cincinnati *Commercial* and after 1890 for the Brooklyn *Standard-Union*. He wrote campaign biographies of William McKinley and Theodore Roosevelt and gave journalistic endorsement to a succession of reform programs and reformist political candidates. "Tall and massively formed, with a large head and snow-white hair and beard," reported an impressed observer near the close of the century, he was "the most familiar figure in Republican National Conventions." He had made the Cincinnati *Commercial* into "one of the most notable political and literary influences of the country."[3] Politicians recognized—and many of them feared—the power of his pen.

Throughout his long career as a political commentator, Halstead held to the theme which he first voiced in 1856—the great mass of the people wanted a clear trial of the great issues, and the politicians denied them a full and fair expression of their opinions. In 1860, Halstead's thesis was that 'King Caucus'—the convention system of choosing candidates and formulating party platforms—was the enemy of popular government. In 1856, he was sure that the trucklers and the temporizers were denying the people the right to make a decision. Once—in 1872—Halstead himself became an active politician. In conjunction with other newspaper men, he sat in the 'smoke-filled room,' which he so generally denounced, and directed the curiously wrought Liberal Republican Party convention. There he received a practical demonstration of the necessity for truckling and compromising, and his convention chose the most unlikely of compromise and coalition candidates, Horace Greeley. The experience led him to stick to his journalistic last thereafter but never caused him to modify his caustic opinions of politicians. Perhaps, indeed, Halstead as a journalist had a vested interest in controversy, in sharply defined issues, and in fiery, news-making campaigns. It was an interest which clashed with the vested interests of politicians in maintaining an even balance, in harmonizing conflicts, in formulating a viable synthesis of the varying concerns of groups and regions in America.

In a sense, 1856 saw the last campaign for many years in which the political parties sought to fulfill their traditional function of making an effective compromise. The issues of the day were heavily loaded with moral content, and the pundits of press and pulpit had succeeded in arousing intense emotions about them. A decade earlier, the historic course of American expansion over the hemisphere had been suddenly halted in the middle of the Mexican War, and Americans had turned to quarrelling over whether the system of slavery or of free labor should control the territory acquired by the onward march of empire. The issue of slavery in Kansas, raised by Stephen A. Douglas in 1854 when he introduced the Kansas-Nebraska Bill, had stimulated the rise of new political opposition groups which, calling themselves Republican, were prepared to launch a national Republican Party. The settlement of Kansas had produced conflict in the territory and, just on the eve of the conventions, the caning of Massachusetts Senator Charles Sumner on the Senate floor and the sack of Lawrence in Kansas, had dramatically accented sectional hatreds.

At the same time that Kansas became a burning question, American filibusters in Central America and a verbal clash with Spain over the treatment of Americans in Cuba called attention to the continued desire of Southern expansionists, 'Young Americans,' and apostles of 'Manifest Destiny' for the annexation of more territory. Opinions and emotions were dividing along sectional lines until even so practical a proposal as a railroad to the Pacific Coast took on moral implications. In addition, the question of the influence of newly arrived immigrants in American life, and the growing strength of the

Catholic Church in hitherto Protestant America excited feelings. An 'American Party', promptly dubbed the "Know-
Nothing Party," had summoned all true patriots to turn back
the threat which foreigners and an alien faith were presumably
making on American traditions. By 1856 the issues and the
emotions were testing the ancient American principle of compromise. That year, to the disgust of Halstead and the agitators
who wanted a clear contest on the moral questions, the parties
succeeded in evading the issues and offered candidates who
were more distinguished for availability than for rigid adherence
to principles. "We feel little interest in the coming campaign,"
moaned Halstead. "If it is to be more a conflict of interests and
factions, with no recognized and defined doctrinal significance,
we had as soon one party would succeed as another."[4]

In Halstead's opinion, Ohio's Salmon P. Chase and Senator
Stephen A. Douglas of Illinois were "the most perfect embodi-
ments of the sentiments of the parties to which they belong."
The nomination of these men would "present in its most pure
and simple form"[5] the questions before the people, while any
politician who would prevent this popular trial by bartering
away principles, injecting immaterial issues, or backing "non-
representative men" would commit a wrong for which there
could be no atonement. Yet, as he looked around, he found
that the friends of James Buchanan and the "discoverers" of
John C. Fremont were vigorously advancing their respective
candidacies, and there was even a willingness, on the part of
Republicans, to enter into a coalition with the Know Nothings.
Under such circumstances, defeat would be desirable. As for
the Democratic Party, Halstead sneered, "we know of nothing
that could be employed to insure its dissolution . . . half so efficient as an administration headed by such a personage as the
Pennsylvania statesman."[6]

Since Halstead was resigned to failure and the compromise
of all principles, he was able to view the conventions of the
parties with a skepticism that bordered on objectivity. He attended the conventions—first the Know Nothing meeting in
Philadelphia on Washington's Birthday and the Republicans'
mass meeting in Pittsburgh. Then the Democrats gathered in
his own Cincinnati, followed by the sparsely attended second,
or northern, Know Nothing convention in New York City, and

after that the full-flowered Republican convention in Philadelphia. From each he sent back to his paper telegraphic accounts
of the proceedings, and followed them with newsletters explor-
ing the events and personalities of the day. Finally, during and
after the meetings, he wrote interpretative editorials on the
conventions and their misdeeds. His newsletters made incisive
comments on the movements in the conventions, caught the
spirit of the crowds, and limned the personalities who strode
the boards for brief appearances or who sat in covert dens to
guide the delegates. He cast new light on the processes of
politics, and made his own small contribution to a growing dis-
illusionment with politicians. He was an able forerunner of
later generations of columnists and commentators.

As the time drew near for the American Party to assemble,
Halstead took a morbid delight in recounting its decadence
and imminent fall. The party was rent by factionalism, and it
was only kept alive, in the journalist's opinion, by "the force of
human perversity." [7] The principles upon which the party was
founded—opposition to foreigners and an excessive patriotism
—had ceased to be a bond of union. Halstead ridiculed the
'Samism' of the party which selected Washington's Birthday as
its meeting date and availed itself of the American Eagle,
George Washington, the patriot fathers, and the flag as party
symbols. "The Pope, the Devil, and SAM are no longer topics
of interest," he reported. Instead, the Americans had been split
into North Americans and South Americans by the slavery
issue. In June 1855, the National Council of the Order of the
Star Spangled Banner had adopted a platform repudiating
slavery extension and favoring the Free-State movement in
Kansas; "South Americans" promptly denounced the national
council, and prepared to move into the nominating convention
with a platform and a program of their own. "SAM," recorded
Halstead, "is actually fading away before the fast colors of
SAMBO'S countenance." [8]

The convention of the Know Nothings bore out Halstead's
predictions. The Southerners came in with determination, withdrew in protest amid scenes of wild confusion, and came back,
their victory won, with renewed declarations of harmony. But
their return only signaled a withdrawal of Northern delegates
who objected to sitting with Louisiana representatives who

came from Catholic constituencies. Moreover, the convention nominated Millard Fillmore, once a Whig President of the United States,[9] and never an avowed advocate of Know Nothing principles. The seceders called for a new convention, and hoped to effect a coalition with the Republicans. The candidate, thought Halstead, was a "man of negatives. . . . His cold, precise manners, selfish character, and trimming disposition, never enlisted an admirer, or aroused a single feeling of enthusiasm. Perpetually in doubt, and as constantly doubted, he would only have arisen in the days of a waning party. . . ."[10] He could not, of course, be elected.

Leaving the Know Nothing convention, Halstead hurried with enthusiasm to Pittsburgh where high-minded men—whose appearance was "calculated to impress the observer with a favorable idea of the influence of free institutions upon the popular character"[11]—were gathering to inaugurate the National Republican Party. These were not the "time-serving pretenders," the "damnable both-sides rogues,"[12] whom he had left in Philadelphia. They were men of "talent, learning and character," with "no manifestations of intolerance or fanaticism," and whose "deliberations were distinguished by a spirit of candor and mutual concessions."[13] At the moment, Halstead was still hopeful that the Republicans, who would meet in formal nominating convention in June, would select Salmon P. Chase for their nominee, and he even had some hope that Chase would meet Stephen A. Douglas on the hustings.

In the three months before the Democrats gathered in Cincinnati, the chances for a positive candidate on a clear-cut platform grew dim. As Halstead noted, the party itself had undergone changes. The "old Jackson Guard" had left the party and been replaced by "fossil Whigs," pro-slavery nullifiers, and disaffected Know Nothings. It had lost its unity and become a "confused jumble of odds and ends of disbanded factions."[14] The petty politicians who ran the party had only contempt for popular opinion, and they sought a candidate who was "neutral in personality and principle."[15] As the time for the convention approached, the chances for either President Franklin Pierce or Senator Douglas grew fainter. Both were too closely connected with the Kansas troubles, and Douglas was, in addition, personally offensive to some of the Southern leaders. "In a high sense, he is no gentleman," reported Halstead. "The Southern gentlemen do not wish to see such a vulgarian in the White House." [16] While a majority of the Southern states chose delegations to Cincinnati pledged to Pierce, there was a strong sentiment against him. Moreover, Virginia's leaders broke the Southern phalanx by deserting Pierce and drawing closer to Pennsylvania's James Buchanan. [17] On the eve of the convention, Buchanan seemed certain of strong Northern support against a divided South.

James Buchanan had been nearly a half century in public life, first as a Federalist and then as a Democrat. He had been a congressman and Senator, a minister to Russia and to Great Britain, and Secretary of State. No candidate had so long or so varied an experience. With it all, as Halstead saw it, "this experienced and veteran camp follower has learned, if nothing else, the benefits of noncommittalism, and the art of holding his dish right side up, whatever may be the direction of the shower." If he had few personal friends, he had also no enemies. "The friends of the weak are weaklings," [18] said the *Commercial's* editorialist, who predicted that Buchanan as President would not obtain the support of the vigorous element in his own party and that the party would dissipate because of his lack of leadership.

Halstead's pre-convention predictions were quickly fulfilled when the Democrats met. The journalist followed the proceedings with glee, recording the arrival of the advance guard of "pimps and prostitutes, political and other gamblers," [19] quoting the pompous fulminations of "Old Bullion" Benton, watching the disorders as disowned Missourians broke into the convention hall, assessing the merits of the conflicts between Hards and Softs from New York. With no interest in the outcome, he promised a full and fair account. "We occupy a wholly independent position, and have no disposition in this case to do otherwise than to write history." [20] So saying he passed judgment on the colorful personalities sweating in the crowded hall, selected the incidents to be described, and determined that the outbursts of enthusiasm were not "genuinely thorough and spontaneous." [21] His account, for all of its bias, was the best that came from the convention, and his readers could follow intelligently the moves which led to the adoption of the "Squatter-

Sovereignty" platform, and the maneuvers which resulted in Buchanan's nomination. His report showed the declining influence of Pierce, the desperate effort to throw Pierce's Southern delegations to Douglas, and the dramatic suddenness of Douglas' withdrawal from the race. And in the end, when Buchanan had won the nomination, Halstead summed up the proceedings with a rhetorical question. "Who knows where he is? He is placed, it is true, upon what is called a 'platform'—a collection of politico-literary absurdities and enormities, in the name of which damnable deeds have been committed, and may be again: but what idea to the people of the Union does the name of James Buchanan suggest?" [22]

Ten days after the Democrats adjourned, the Republicans gathered in Philadelphia for their first national convention. Enroute to the meeting, Halstead stopped in New York to observe the bolting Know Nothings, who had denounced Fillmore. It was "the fag end of a fag end." [23] The meeting, he correctly gauged, was designed to offer a coalition to the Republicans— a proposition which, in Halstead's opinion, would be a "fatal poison." If individual Know Nothings wished to join the Republicans, they should first be purified—"washed in vinegar and rubbed with sulphur" [24]—and then admitted only to the lower ranks. He was more than disgusted with New York's Edwin D. Morgan, chairman of the Republican executive committee, who had invited the bolters to fuse with the Republicans. It gave hope to the remnants of the American Party that they might name the Vice-President on the Republican ticket.

Coalition, in fact, seemed to Halstead as great a crime against the people as the neutral nomination of the non-committal Buchanan. "A party can afford to be beaten," he remarked sententiously, "but it cannot afford to dishonor its principles." [25] Yet as the day approached for the Republican convention, he saw increasing evidences that principles would be sacrificed to expediency. Not only was there danger that the Republicans would coalesce with the Know Nothings, there was also the danger that old Whiggery would rise to dominate the new party. Moreover, Salmon P. Chase's chances faded, and practical politicians were taking over the movement. In Massachusetts the Know Nothing Nathaniel P. Banks, speaker of the House of Representatives, and Senator Henry Wilson had "discovered" John C. Fremont and brought him forth as a candidate. Fremont was Thomas Hart Benton's son-in-law and had won notice, even notoriety, in California but had had no political experience. Veteran Jacksonian Francis Preston Blair, deserting the Democratic Party to preside over the birth pains of the new Republican, had joined the Fremont movement. At the same time, "Congressional president-makers" [26] with Whig antecedents were preparing to foist the venerable Justice John McLean upon the party. The prospects for principles and for a real trial of the issues were poor indeed.

Murat Halstead made no pretense of objectivity as he reported the meeting of the Republicans. His indifference to the result, however, led him to give a less biased account than he had accorded the Democrats. He found the personalities interesting—Henry S. Lane's "westernisms," Blair's ill-fitting false teeth which turn out to be real, Robert Emmett's Irish brogue and ready wit—and he described them dramatically. He caught the color of the convention and understood the significance of parliamentary moves. He reported carefully the efforts to make McLean the nominee and the ill-judged act of his sponsors in withdrawing him. Yet, even as he did so, he caught some of the spirit of the convention. Fremont, he knew, was as negative as Buchanan, as inappropriate a choice as Fillmore. Moreover, he could not forget, or let his readers forget, that the candidate parted his hair in the middle. He could only account for the enthusiasm for Fremont on grounds that approached mysticism. "It seemed, and I do not make the comparison irrelevantly, that a popular instinct, such as sometimes, on great occasions, leaps chasms in logic—for instance, in the case of calling George Washington to be Commander-in-Chief of the American armies of the Revolution—that such an instinct had found in Fremont the man for the times." [27]

The mysticism which thus found so involved an expression was not completely foreign to Murat Halstead, or even to the America of 1856. He was a competent observer of the political scene, and a caustic commentator on the ways of politicians. His reports of the conventions which offered Fillmore, Buchanan, and Fremont to the American electorate had an incisive quality and make a useful and fresh source for an understanding of the efforts of politicians to stay the coming civil war. But underlying the cold realism of the reporter there lay a mystic belief, shared by all who partook of American traditions, that the judgment of the people was sound, that the "ability of the masses for self-government" could be trusted, and that right principles would triumph if only the politicians dared to "present an important issue in a direct form for political agitation and settlement."[28] It was the basic faith of American democracy.

Despite the high significance of conventions in the history of American political parties, scholars have given those of 1856 only cursory attention. The Republican meetings have formed an incidental part of Ruhl Jacob Bartlett, *John C. Fremont and the Republican Party* (Columbus, 1930); Allan Nevins, *Fremont, Pathmarker of the West* (New York, 1939); and Francis P. Weisenburger, *The Life of John McLean: A Politician on the United States Supreme Court* (Columbus, 1937). The Know-Nothings are in Ray Allen Billington, *The Protestant Crusade, 1800-1860: A Study of the Origins of American Nativism* (New York, 1938), and W. Darrell Overdyke, *The Know-Nothing Party in the South* (Baton Rouge, 1950). Roy F. Nichols, *Disruption of American Democracy* (New York, 1948), gives some attention to the Democrats, who are also treated in George F. Milton, *The Eve of Conflict: Stephen A. Douglas and the Needless War* (Boston and New York, 1934). Although students of the period have followed carefully Halstead's accounts of the conventions of 1860, they have neglected his incisive comments on the conventions of 1856.

In bringing these notes on the conventions together, we have included a few telegraphic reports and supplemented them with Halstead's detailed letters from the conventions, and his editorials written either from the convention city or immediately after his return to his desk. In some cases we have used earlier editorials to furnish a background for the conventions and the nominees. We have omitted redundant or irrelevant material, corrected obvious errors in printing, supplied first names or initials for delegates and candidates mentioned, and changed punctuation, paragraphing, and capitalization to conform to modern usage.

Madison, Wisconsin   W. B. H.
Fall, 1960

                                                        R. F.

First Know Nothing Convention

‡ ‡ ‡

AMERICAN NATIONAL CONVENTION

Philadelphia, February 22

The American National Convention assembled this morning in the National Hall, Market Street.[1] Isaac Hazel-Hurst, of Philadelphia, was chosen temporary chairman. Credentials are being examined now, and much time will be occupied by deciding the various claims to seats by the Pennsylvania delegation.

The committee on organization reported as permanent officers: Ephraim Marsh, of New Jersey, President, and twenty-four vice-presidents, one from each state represented. . . .

Reassembling this evening, permanent officers were elected and took their seats. The committee on credentials submitted majority and minority reports—the former reporting in favor of the Edie delegates, the latter, signed by Southern members, refusing to recognize delegates from any council repudiating the platform of 1855, or the 12th section of that platform.

An animated discussion ensued upon the admission of the Edie delegates.[2]

[1]

February 23

The national convention was a scene of the utmost excitement all the morning.[3] Threats of secession by the Southern members were boldly proclaimed. . . .

After a stormy debate, the vote was taken on the majority report of the credentials committee, and it was adopted—yeas 88, nays 45.

General Joseph G. Pickett, of Tennessee, denounced the course pursued by the North, and left the convention, declining to take any further part in its actions.

Mr. John D. Imboden, of Virginia, entreated the Southern members not to go then, and perhaps in a few hours they would find many to go with them. . . .

After a speech from Governor Richard K. Call, of Florida, in which he announced his intention of leaving, Mr. E. B. Bartlett, of Kentucky, made an earnest appeal not to desert their friends in the convention, and made a motion to adjourn till the 3rd of July. A motion to lay it on the table was made, and the yeas and nays being demanded, the roll was called, the delegates generally giving their reasons for their votes, so that the whole day was occupied by long speeches, and at six o'clock the vote was announced—yeas 128, nays 73. A scene of wild confusion ensued, the members shouting out twenty different motions at the same time. A motion to adjourn till Monday morning finally prevailed.

February 25, Morning session[4]

Resolution offered that the national convention has no authority to prescribe a platform of principles for this convention, and we will nominate no candidate for President and Vice-President who is not in favor of interdicting the introduction of slavery north of 36-30.

A motion to lay it on the table carried—yeas 141, nays 59.

Mr. William G. Brownlow moved that the convention proceed to the nomination of candidates for President and Vice-President, forthwith, and moved previous question. Call sustained by a unanimous vote.

THE CLOSING SCENES – THE BOLT AND THE NOMINATION – AN INTERESTING ROW

The motion to go into the nomination of candidates for President and Vice-President was made by the famous Parson Brownlow, of Tennessee, and carried—yeas 151, nays 51.[5] The New York *Tribune*'s reporter says of this motion:

It had all the Southern votes, all of New York, half of Pennsylvania, a quarter of Ohio, two-thirds of Massachusetts and Wisconsin, and part of Illinois; Connecticut, Rhode Island, Ohio, Pennsylvania and Massachusetts furnished the votes against it.

Speech of Perkins, of Connecticut

When the vote was declared, Mr. Edmund Perkins, of Connecticut, rose, and after intense confusion and excitement for some moments, commanded full attention. He had little now to say for the North, only he should speak a little more in earnest. Gentlemen of the South had before stated their position; he would now state that of the minority. . . . There are two great questions before the minds of the people of this country; one is the issue of Americanism, which is simply the reform of naturalization laws; that we are agreed in. But, Sir, there is another question which must be an element in the coming canvass, in which the people are deeply interested; that is, the question of what shall be done about restoration of freedom to Kansas; what shall be done to compensate the North for the loss of that guaranty for freedom which has been stolen from them. The South admits that the Kansas-Nebraska Act was a fraud; they cannot and dare not deny it. This question cannot be ignored; it must be met; no candidate can be nominated whose position on that question is doubtful. You must declare yourselves in this issue. The South would have seceded from this convention had the twelfth section been repealed purely and simply; they owned it; and now will they expect us to do less than they would have done? The free territory was ours by compact, by argument, by the most solemn sanction. You have stolen it from us by the treachery of Northern men; you admit that you ought to restore to us our own, but you refuse to do it. This is a practical question—it is no abstraction. Now what is your chance on your platform—which means nothing, or is a pro-slavery one? You cannot carry the South—not a single state, in any event. We could sweep the whole North on our platform, and you do your best to defeat us; you commit a suicide. You pretend that we are to be sold out to the Black Republicans; I know no such. But we shall—those of us who are driven away from you—go for our principles—our Americanism, our freedom; and the Republicans of the country will join with us. . . .

No man on this floor believes a dissolution of the Union is possible; it is an idle dream—a silly fantasy. The Union is in no danger, and no man thinks it is. If you won't give us what we demand, we will take it ourselves, and the Union will not be dissolved. Every president from Washington to James K. Polk has done all we claim shall be done now; and yet the Union has not suffered. You cannot carry this Union on stars and stripes and the American eagle without something reliable to stand upon. We can save Americanism and secure freedom to the territories together, and we will do it. We are not going to sizzle and fade out; we are going out as the American Party of the Union, standing upon the platform we have presented this morning, and calling a convention for the whole Union upon our platform. We have got a Fugitive Slave law; we obey it; but we will not hunt niggers; there is no gentleman on this floor, North or South, who will engage in this business of hunting niggers—not one of you. We in Connecticut don't think much of this law— we don't think it Constitutional, but we do not intend to dissolve the Union because of it. . . . Mr. Perkins concluded his most admirable and eloquent speech with the announcement that all delegates of Connecticut, and others from the free states who agree with them, would now retire from the convention. New Hampshire, Massachusetts, and Rhode Island, and a portion of the delegations from Ohio, Illinois, Iowa, and Pennsylvania followed.

After more speaking in this line, a nominating ballot was taken (each delegate naming his candidate) and the following was the result: Millard Fillmore of New York, 71; George Law of New York, 27; Garrett Davis of Kentucky, 13; John McLean of Ohio, 7; Robert F. Stockton of New Jersey, 8; Sam Houston of Texas, 6; John Bell of Tennessee, 5; Kenneth Rayner of North Carolina, 2; Erastus Brooks of New York, 2; Lewis D. Campbell of Ohio, 1; and John M. Clayton of Delaware, 1.

Mr. J. C. Knight of Rhode Island voted for Fillmore, and no other New England delegate voted. New York voted: Fillmore, 9; Law, 15; Houston, 6; Brooks, 1. New Jersey swallowed Commodore Stockton entire. Pennsylvania (that remained in) divided between Governor William F. Johnston, McLean, and Fillmore. The few Ohio men remaining voted for Davis, and, with scarce an exception, the entire balance of the slave states voted for Fillmore.

The result of the voting was hailed with great satisfaction by the South and the New York Fillmore men. The former had secured a better guaranty than any platform—than even the twelfth section—that their policy was to be protected by the great National American Party. But the Law men drooped sadly; their bubble was burst; men had voted against them with his dinners and wine in their stomachs, to say nothing of his money in their pockets.

The convention then, at 4 o'clock, took a recess till 5.

When the Northern men seceded they were derided with insults by the Southern men and doughfaces of the North. Cries of "Good Riddance," "Glad you are gone," "Black Republicans," etc., were heard in different parts of the house.

Evening session

The convention was called to order at 5 o'clock. Parson Brownlow, of Tennessee, moved that Governor Richard Call of Florida, Mr. Percy Walker of Alabama, and all other Southern gentlemen, who had felt disgusted last week and retired, be invited to come back into the church now. [Laughter, and cries of "Good."]

Governor Call came in, and he and Parson Brownlow fell into each other's arms, and indulged in a loving embrace. Governor

Call made a speech, saying that he was glad to come back again, and join with his brethren whom he had left hastily, but not in anger. He said if he got a standard bearer that suited him he would go in for him.

Mr. Walker also made confession of his wanderings, and returned to the fold of the Know Nothing Southern Church. He said he could not allow his love for Americanism or the Union to make him untrue to the South. . . . But this morning's session had been one of reform and returning good sense, and therefore Mr. Walker kindly and condescendingly came back. . . .

A Delaware delegate withdrew the name of John M. Clayton as a candidate for the presidency. Mr. Brooks' name was also withdrawn. It was stated that Commodore Stockton was no commodore at all—only plain Robert F. Stockton.

Then was had the formal ballot for candidate for President, and the result was as follows—the voting being, not by individual delegates, as in the informal ballot, but by states, according to their federal representation: Millard Fillmore, 179; George Law, 24; Kenneth Rayner, 14; John McLean, 13; Garrett Davis, 10; and Sam Houston, 3; total, 243; necessary to a choice, 122.

Millard Fillmore, of New York, was then declared the nominee of the National American Convention for President of the United States.

Great excitement ensued, and the convention was in a tremendous uproar for some moments. Erastus Brooks, of New York, returned thanks to the South in behalf of Mr. Fillmore. The Law men were terribly down in the mouth.

Governor Call, of Florida; Kenneth Rayner, of North Carolina; Andrew J. Donelson, of Tennessee; and several others were named for the vice-presidency. . . .

A scene of great tumult ensued; and at last the voting for Vice-President commenced. The struggle was chiefly between Donelson and Walker.

The result of the ballot for Vice-President was as follows: A. J. Donelson of Tennessee, 181; Percy Walker of Mississippi, 8; H. J. Gardner of Massachusetts, 8; and Kenneth Rayner of North Carolina, 8. Donelson received the unanimous nomination for the vice-presidency.

Donelson spoke as follows:

I lack words to express my thanks for the vote with which you have honored me. I have not sought it, and I shall not decline it, although during Mr. Fillmore's administration he did not agree with us, yet he said we ought to be more Americanized. I have many letters from him, and they all breathe the warmest attachment to the Constitution and the Union. I live at the South, and I am owner of more than an hundred slaves, and I like the institution as warmly as any man born south of Mason and Dixon's line. But while I claim every thing for the South, I am not the less sensitive of the claims of the North. We ask for nothing for the South that we are not willing to grant to the North. I left the Democratic Party.

A Voice: It left you, Mr. Donelson. [Loud laughter.]

Mr. Donelson: I could not agree with the sectional policy of the present administration. Mr. Donelson further said that if General Andrew Jackson, Mr. Daniel Webster, and Mr. Henry Clay were alive, they would be on the American platform. He would have preferred that some one else should have received the nomination, and promised that whatever of energy, talent, or good will he possessed should be given to the cause.

* * *

THE NEW CODE OF KNOW NOTHINGISM

Some curiosity is naturally felt as to the new "American Platform of Principles" which was, on Thursday, adopted by the national council at Philadelphia.[6] This thing is, as the world moves, of very little importance, and it is only necessary to say that the principal feature of it is, that the slavery question is dodged entirely, while it contains the usual amount of humbug rhetoric in the peculiar style, with which all persons who have heard Know Nothing stump speeches or Pap Taylor[7] editorials, are sufficiently familiar. After an "humble acknowledgment, to the Supreme Being who rules the universe," and a puff of the Union, the platform tells us that "Americans *must* rule America," and that native born citizens should be selected in preference of those naturalized, for all offices. The fifth section is in favor of a close paraphrase of the form of the oath of naturalization, and is opposed to the *Higher Law* thus:

"No person should be selected for political station (whether of native or foreign birth), who recognizes any allegiance or obligation of any description to any foreign prince, potentate or power, or who refuses to recognize the federal and state constitutions (each within its sphere) as paramount to all other laws, as rules of political action."

The sixth section favors the "unqualified recognition and maintenance of the reserved rights of the several states." The seventh section is an endorsement of the Douglas doctrine of squatter sovereignty, while the eighth goes in for an enforcement of the principle that no state or territory can admit others than natives or those regularly naturalized, to the right of suffrage. The ninth section favors fixing the term of probation previous to naturalization at twenty-one years, and objects to foreign paupers. The tenth section opposes the union of Church and State. The eleventh instalment of doctrine advocates economy in the use of public money. The twelfth is for the maintenance of laws until they are repealed. The thirteenth section pitches into the administration for removing Know Nothings from office and deprecates the repeal of the Missouri Compromise, because it reopened sectional controversy, and asserts that the administration was very wrong in removing Judge Greene C. Bronson from the New York collectorship. The fourteenth article of faith advocates building up the Know Nothing Party by "eschewing all sectional questions and uniting upon those purely national." Herein we also have an elucidation of the process of becoming members of the order—all natives who avow the principles "herein before stated," and "who will subscribe their names to this platform." Does this mean that the oaths of the order are dispensed with? The fifteenth and last section is thus brief: "A free and open discussion of all political principles embraced in our platform." Can this mean that the meetings of the order are to be open to the public? This platform is certainly the most appropriate one that could have been devised for the Know Nothings. It is merely, and veritably *nothingness sectionalized*—or, if we may be allowed a figurative form of expression—it is a weak broth of the "*goose* question" prepared without seasoning, the temperature of which is to be regulated by the breath of those who are disposed to swallow it, or have it otherwise administered, as a political prescription. So mild a medicine will not raise the dead.

Mr. Fillmore–What Is He?

Several able editors in different sections of the United States are laboring to find reasons why Mr. Fillmore should not be supported as a candidate for the office of president.[8] The Washington *Union* discovers him to be an Abolitionist, and publishes a letter of his, written in 1838, wherein he declares himself in favor of receiving Abolition petitions, opposed to the annexation of Texas as a slave state, and in favor of the abolition of the internal slave trade, and of slavery in the District of Columbia, insisting that unless he has publicly recanted these opinions or is entitled to the benefit of the statute of limitations upon their expression, he is not fit to be trusted in times like the present. The New York *Tribune,* on the contrary, makes him out a pro-slavery man, thinks that if elected, he would be found an inveterate enemy to freedom, and that he has been tried by slavery and "not found wanting." These comprise the extremes of opinion. They are nearly as wide as the poles apart; and it is a matter of some consequence to know whether, during the canvass that is to come, the claims of Mr. Fillmore to the presidency are to be discussed upon this issue. Most assuredly we hope not.

It is a better reason against Mr. Fillmore that . . . there is any doubt as to where he stands. In these times an equivocal position is no position. It is one that will win no confidence, excite no admiration, and enlist no support. It is useless to talk of what he was—the question is, what is he? And the mere fact that this inquiry cannot be satisfactorily answered is conclusive against him. There is no body of the people of the United States—or at least but a very small one—who desire, in this contest, to elect a man of negatives. Yet such a man Mr. Fillmore always was, and always will be. It is in his nature, and he cannot avoid it if he would. He was a tolerable party follower, but never possessed the qualifications of a leader of the people. The consequence has been that he was always dead weight for his party to carry. He never aided the presidential ticket upon which he was elected a particle. Whiggery in the State of New York groaned under him, and bore him as a burden, in all state elections where he was a candidate. His cold, precise manners, selfish character, and trimming disposition, never enlisted an admirer, nor aroused a single feeling of enthusiasm. Perpetually in doubt, and as constantly doubted, he could only have arisen in the days of a waning party, and must necessarily be insignificant in that to which he is attached, precisely in proportion to its real health and power.

PROTESTS

The seceders from the American convention have published the following address:[9]

> We . . . find ourselves compelled to dissent from the opinions avowed by that body, and holding as we do, the opinion, that the restoration of the Missouri Compromise, demanded by a majority of the whole people, is a redress of an undeniable wrong . . . and we hold that the admission into the national council, and nominating convention, of the delegates from Louisiana, representing Roman Catholic constituents, absolved every true American from all obligations to sustain the actions of either of said bodies. We have, therefore, withdrawn from the nominating convention, refusing to participate in the proposed nominations, and now address ourselves to the Americans of the country, and . . . we propose to the Americans in all the states to assemble in their several state organizations, and elect delegates to meet in convention in the city of New York, on Thursday, the 12th day of next June, for the purpose of nominating candidates for president and vice-president of the United States. . . .

Sixty-seven delegates were present including eight from New York, but the latter did not sign the protest.

That portion of the delegation from New York who opposed the nomination of Fillmore have prepared the following protest:[10]

> We . . . protest against the nomination by that convention upon the following grounds:

1st. The nominee is not a member of the American Party; he has never been inside of a council room, and no act of his life, no word spoken or line written by him, which we have any knowledge of, indicates that he has any sympathy with the party, or would carry out its principles.

2d. His nomination we regard as an utter betrayal of the American movement—a traitorous attempt to wrest it from its purpose, and make it minister to the selfish ambition of the leaders and demagogues of the dead organizations of the past.

3d. He has forced upon the State of New York by Southern votes against the wish of our state delegates, and from those states which no man pretends can carry their vote for an American President.

4th. He was forced upon the State of New York against the express wish of a large majority of the members of the legislature, against the express wish of two-thirds of our delegates in the convention.

5th. He was not nominated by a majority of the states. Several states were permitted to cast their votes through a single delegate, who cast the whole number of votes which his state would have entitled him, had the delegation been full. In several instances such votes were cast for parties who had previously protested against the proceedings, and retired from the convention.

CHAPTER 2

Republican National Mass Meeting

‡   ‡   ‡

[*In the following section the editors have summarized the major events of the Republican Mass Meeting at Pittsburgh. The information appeared in the Cincinnati* COMMERCIAL *of February 23 and 25, 1856.*]

DETAILS OF THE MEETING

ON FEBRUARY 22 and 23, 1856, delegates of twenty-four state Republican parties met at Pittsburgh, Pennsylvania, to complete the formal organization of a new national political party. The vast majority of the delegates came from Northern states while only a few represented the slave states of Missouri, Texas, Kentucky, Delaware, Maryland, Virginia, South Carolina, and Tennessee.

Due to the late arrival of trains bringing the New York, Pennsylvania, and New Jersey delegations, the convention accomplished little of its formal work on the first day except the election of Francis P. Blair, a Maryland slave-holder, as president of the convention. "Great applause" greeted Blair's unanimous election. The remainder of this day was devoted to speechmaking. Horace Greeley of New York, Joshua Giddings of

Ohio, several preachers, and others addressed the convention. The Reverend John Lovejoy, of Illinois, urged that the Kansas affair be settled and pleaded for "war to the knife." Greeley warned the delegates that the party should not be one of caution. Giddings rose to speak amid cheers and described the progress the "cause" had made, which would be consummated by the present generation. All was not harmonious, however, as Zachariah Chandler, of Michigan, charged that two Republican Ohio members of Congress lacked backbone during the contest for the election of the speaker of the House.

On the morning of the second day, as the committees were not ready to report, one delegate from each state, each allotted ten minutes, addressed the convention.

General Silas M. Burrows, of New York, explained the difficulties Republicans encountered in his state in organizing a party. It was easy to form a small party on the slavery question but concessions must be made in order to form a large party. He thought a large proportion of the American Party could be brought to the Republican cause.

George W. Julian, of Indiana, reported for the committee on organization which advised: (1) the formation of an executive national committee composed of one man from each state, and (2) the assembling of a national convention at Harrisburg, Pennsylvania, on June 17, to nominate a presidential candidate. The delegates changed the meeting place to Philadelphia.

The committee on declarations presented a fifty-page report mostly devoted to Kansas. With nine cheers the delegates unanimously resolved: (1) to repeal all laws for the introduction of slavery into the territories, (2) to admit Kansas as a free state, and (3) to overthrow the Administration for its reprehensible conduct of the Kansas question.

The convention adjourned.

*   *   *

THE MEETING AT PITTSBURGH

The mass meeting of Republicans at Pittsburgh on the 22d and 23d inst., was one of those assemblages whose appearance is calculated to impress the observer with a favorable idea of the influence of free institutions upon the popular character, and to afford the friends of a government of the people a cheering prognostic of the continuance of that which has already been the parent of so many benefits to our fathers and ourselves.[1] Gathered from various parts of the Union, and embodying a larger amount of talent, learning and character, than has convened in any similar political body in this Union for many years, its deliberations were distinguished by a spirit of candor and mutual concession, and, we doubt not, its acts, while they will, in general, be met by the approval of the Republican body of the North, will present nothing at which judicious and impartial men at the South will feel themselves entitled to complain. Claiming for the North, at the hands of the Union, political rights of which it has been unjustly deprived, there were no manifestations of intolerance or fanaticism; and we do not recollect to have heard a single expression coming from a northern man in whose tone or temper even a pro-slavery man from the South would find any real cause of offense.

The proceedings of the body, so far as it is necessary to understand their spirit, have been already published. Resolutions and a very lengthy address have not yet come to hand. These will, doubtless, in due time be accessible. In this case, however, the functions performed by the body do not consist in its literature. There was no candidate to nominate nor platform to construct. The object was to inaugurate the commencement of a REPUBLICAN PARTY, by laying the basis for future action by Republicans in a national capacity. This was accomplished when the four or five hundred representatives of a popular conviction met in the hall and looked in each others' faces. That recognized unanimity of sentiment, which drew them from all parts of the Union upon the same errand, was the primary and organic fact of the occasion. The robustness of the career of the party in coming time was evinced by the unanimity of those who had come together to assist at its birth. There was apparent none of that disposition to "realize" as rapidly as possible upon the capital on hand, that is so striking a feature in several of the younger political organizations of the country, testifying strongly to infantile decrepitude and premature old age. There was little said about presidents or presidential candidates, and much about bringing the Republic back to the condition in which it was when it passed from the hands of the men of the Revolution—a sacred trust, for the keeping of which we are responsible.

This is a brief view of what struck us as the general character and tendency of the body at Pittsburgh, of which we were an observer. So far, in the movement, there is much to commend. Some things also there were that did not strike us so favorably. These we shall allude to from time to time, as occasion may offer.

CHAPTER 3

Democratic Convention

‡   ‡   ‡

CANDIDATES AND ISSUES

Pierce and Buchanan War

THE FRANKLIN PIERCE and James Buchanan partisans are, as
the season advances for active operations in all departments of
business, political and agricultural, warming in their war har-
ness, and the fight grows hot and strong. . . .[1] The Pierce and
Buchanan quarrel began at the moment when it became apparent to the particular friends of each, that the President and
the Minister to England would be rival aspirants before the
Cincinnati convention, for its elevation to the candidacy for the
highest office within the gift of a free people. The strength of
Pierce consisted in "possession," in the enormous amount of
patronage at his disposal, in the fact that he presided in the
grand central office of the wire-workers of the best drilled party
in the country, and was commander-in-chief of office holders.
Buchanan's strength unquestionably was and is in the fact that
during the political wars which were inaugurated by Stephen A.

[16]

Douglas, Pierce & Co., and in which the Democratic Party was torn in pieces and humbled from the position in the "pride of place" which it held when Pierce moved from the little white house at Concord to the big one at Washington, he was absent from the country. He was, therefore, not identified with the outrage of the repeal of the Missouri Compromise, or the humbug of squatter sovereignty. He had not ostensively fitted to himself the new style of democracy, and was in consequence, as was apparent the moment the eye rested on him, the man for leader of the Democrats who had been offended at Pierce and would be satisfied with negative qualities merely, in their presidential candidate. He seemed to offer in himself a temple of refuge for those who had assisted to elect Pierce, but had backed out when that official proceeded to such extremities with the "nigger business," and yet were afraid to cut loose from the party and go with the Republicans. He was the personification of evasion, the embodiment of an inducement to dodge. This was known thoroughly by every intelligent politician, and the only question was—when and how should it be authoritatively proclaimed? A Buchanan movement was started in this city. The intention doubtless was to make this move a matter of great significance. It was in the city wherein the convention was to be held; and the time selected for the demonstration was thought to be favorable to the production of a sensation. But the meeting was small, and its effect, nothing. The platform which was introduced smoothed over the "nigger business," but in spite of all precautions there was a nigger in that very timber; and the discovery of and discussion about this incorrigible colored person was the feature of the occasion. In the reports of the meeting, given by all the papers next morning, the nigger loomed up, casting his portentous shadow over the platform of platitudes prepared to meet the favor of the placid Mr. Buchanan. It was plain that the distinguished gentleman from Africa couldn't be dodged. . . .

Mr. Buchanan

Has been received by great crowds of friends at New York and Philadelphia.[2] He has been a very respectable and gentlemanly representative of our country at the British court, but has not accomplished anything specially calling for splendid ovations or national gratitude. It is well known that he has returned home particularly to look after his chances for the presidency, and as an aspirant for that position he has been multitudinously received. The indications are, however, that it would have been better policy for him to have remained abroad. The great gathering of the party crows who croaked and squeaked at his landing, will not benefit him. There is too large a flock of birds who eat the game that others kill, following him, hoping, at last, to spoil the slain who may drop along his path. But they are birds of evil omen, and the indications are that his own corpse will be one of the first feasted upon. PIERCE and DOUGLAS are the mighty hunters who are waiting in ambush for the "Old Buck" of Pennsylvania. The manner in which the "nigger in the wood-pile" was introduced to Mr. Buchanan at New York, is somewhat amusing. A great crowd had collected at the Everett House, where Mr. B. was stopping, and he was called out, and among other things said:

"I have been for years abroad in a foreign land, and I like the noise of the democracy. [Applause.] My heart responds to the acclamations of the noble citizens of this favored country. I have been abroad in other lands; I have witnessed arbitrary power; I have contemplated the people of other countries; but there is no country under God's heavens where a man feels equal to his fellow man except in the United States. [Enthusiastic applause, and cries of "good, Old Buck."] And if you could feel how despotism looks on, how jealous the despotic powers of the world are of our glorious institutions, you would cherish the Constitution and the Union to your hearts, next to your belief in the Christian religion. [Applause.] The Bible for heaven, and the Constitution of your country for earth." [Renewed applause.]

A Voice: What about slavery?

Mr. Buchanan did not say "What about slavery." His strength, his friends hold, is in his silence on that very subject. But he will find that in both North and South he must meet the question, "What about slavery?" It is the question.

The Honorable Mister Douglas

Beaten by Lyman Trumbull, snubbed by John J. Crittenden, demolished by William H. Seward, and disgraced by James Lane, the *Honorable* Stephen A. Douglas is in a fair way to become the most appropriate possible representation of Southern pro-slavery democracy in the coming presidential campaign.[3] An exposed political empyric; a dishonest truckler for unsound popularity; a false pretender to notions of honor, and a foulmouthed bully self-convicted of cowardice, though a coat of whitewash a foot in thickness would not cause him to pass for a gentleman, it cannot be denied that he will make a most admirable candidate. We hold up multitudinous hands for his nomination. The party should take him—certify him—swear he is what he professes to be. It will not be the first time that an ill-conditioned ape has been exalted to a deity—probably not the last.

Frauds upon the People

We have, on previous occasions, expressed the opinion that Mr. Salmon P. Chase and Mr. Douglas, or their political equivalents, are the persons whom the present condition of sentiment among the people indicates as the proper candidates for the presidency at the coming election.[4] An examination, without prejudice, of the field of our politics can lead to no other conclusion than that, by their characters, standing and antecedents, these gentlemen, more entirely than any other that can be selected, embody the issue now presented to the citizens of this Union for settlement. Their nomination would open that issue fairly, and we need scarcely go beyond their personal history to find it and the organic principles to which it is allied, combined with all the light that is necessary to render the discussion full and the result satisfactory. Left to itself, popular sentiment would, we are convinced, persevere in this direction until it had secured a complete and satisfactory settlement of the great question of American politics—a consummation than which nothing can be more desirable.

It is unfortunate that, under the inducement of the rewards which industrial avocations offer to every species of activity, the politics of the country have, in a great degree, fallen into the hands of individuals who have proved themselves worthless for any other purpose; and as whoever chooses so to do may become a politician, it is not remarkable that what efficiency there is in the profession is nearly always turned in the wrong direction. There is nothing for which your politician by trade has a more profound contempt than the people—nothing for whose sentiments he has less respect, or of whose views he is more entirely unconscious . . .

While the people have been making up their minds in one direction, the politicians have been making up theirs in another, and the masses on both sides are, to all present appearance, destined to be misled by those who hold in their hands the party organizations. It is not probable that, upon either part, the presidential canvass will present the true issue or the true candidates. Measures are in progress to divest it of every particle of its significance. In tender consideration of his interests, the politician is ever a trimmer—ever ready, by a sale of himself, to realize upon the capital he has acquired. He is especially in favor of third candidacies and compromise men, and if there is anything to which he has a peculiar reluctance, it is to meet his own principles square in the face. In this case, the representative men upon both sides are to be slaughtered under the most ridiculous of all pretences—that in consequence of their firm advocacy of the principles avowed by the several parties to which they belong, they have incurred a portion of personal unpopularity, which will stand in the way of their success. In heaven's name, if this is not the offer of a premium upon dough-faces,[5] what is it? . . .

Administration Party's Change of Front

Facts are being developed and events taking place which, to all appearance, are destined to open a new phase in our national politics, and give an additional significance to the great question, "Is the Union in future to be governed by a SOUTHERN or a **NATIONAL** policy?"[6] The issue is not merely to be, "Shall slavery be extended into the now free territories of the public domain?" but, "Are wars of conquest to be undertaken with a view to the acquisition of new lands whereon to plant the germ of human servitude; and is our government to become the backer and patron of those buccaneering expeditions that, to the eternal disgrace of the civilization and Christianity which we profess, are perpetrating deeds of piracy and murder upon communities with which we, as a nation, are at peace, upon no better pretence than that they are wars of conquest against a barbarous people, to demonstrate the beauties of American freedom, and carry forward in its triumphant career 'our manifest destiny' . . . ?"

Such are the offences against justice that have been committed by the creatures of the government in Kansas, and such the crimes that have been permitted in that country, that there are doubtless many who dread to go before the people upon an issue made directly upon the Kansas policy of the administration. It is feared that a minute and systematic exposure of what has there been done with the permission of the executive, such as would take place during a presidential campaign, would cover the party with disgrace and secure its discomfiture. . . . To get rid of the Kansas issue, therefore, by men with the sagacity of Douglas, has become advisable. . . . Central American affairs given a prominent position in the discussion of the Senate, England and its interference talked of, and the war trumpet blown against that power, and the Panama massacre, manifest destiny, and the necessity for a transit across the Isthmus, made the subjects of Senatorial declamation and cabinet discussion. . . .

This practical admission by the leaders of the party that they cannot hope to conquer under the Kansas standard, and this desperate essay to change the form of the issue now before the American people, is a matter for profound reflection. By its means we can gain a partial idea of the depths of crime to which politicians are ready to descend in order to secure the means to climb to power. The amount of success that is destined to attend the movement, it is now impossible to estimate. To avoid the disgrace which has followed the commission of one series of crime by entering upon another and a greater, is an expedient which, it would seem, none but men in the most desperate circumstances would be willing to adopt. If they fear to meet a Northern sense of justice and love of the right, in the one case, how will they contrive to do it in another? We do not believe that the people of the Northern states of the Union are now ready, or can be induced by party discipline in future to give their votes in the elevation to power of an administration pledged to the violation of all laws, human and divine, all ideas of justice and sentiments of humanity, for the purpose of manufacturing slave states to keep up a Southern preponderance in this confederacy.

What Old Bullion Says

Colonel Thomas Hart Benton has been called on by many gentlemen, at his parlor in the Broadway Hotel.[7] He is electioneering hard and hot for Buchanan, and is death and woe on Pierce and Douglas. He says:

"This administration is most weak and corrupt, sir—corrupt and weak, sir. The President don't know his own mind for one hour, sir—not for one hour. Look at our foreign relations. There is more danger of the peace of the world being disturbed than you are aware, sir, more than you are aware of, sir.

"The passions of the people are fearfully aroused, sir—fearfully aroused. Mention the name of Douglas and every bad passion is aroused—every one aroused, sir. He is a political filibuster, sir, he could not carry a free state. The North is incensed, very justly incensed at his conduct, sir. This thing of slavery agitation was all settled sir, until he broke it up. The angry feeling of the North is very just, sir.

"As for Buchanan—never a leading man in any high sense, sir—but a man of fair talents, and a very pure man in both his public and private life, sir. He is a man of peace, sir—eminently a man of peace. The effect of his nomination would be to restore peace to the country, sir."

CONVENTION

The Coming Convention

Delegates to the coming national Democratic convention—outside and inside, male and female have for several days been making their appearance in the city, and giving an unusually busy appearance to the hotels and places of public resort.[8] The herd also of buzzards and camp-followers—pimps and prostitutes, political and other gamblers, that are inseparable from such events, are showing themselves and preparing to enter upon their several vocations. Party leaders are putting their heads together in out of-the-way places, laying plans to forestall the action of the assembly, and gather into their own hands the means to control the nominations, or to sell out at the best possible price to those whose prospects seem better than their own. Calculators are canvassing the preferences of the different delegates and endeavoring to construct prognostics from the result; while the immediate friends of the several candidates are running hither and thither, striving by new combinations to defeat the plans of their adversaries. In the meantime, the city seems like a great political exchange. Rumors of all kinds are flying in every direction, and the prices of stocks cannot be more variable than the standing of candidates with different times and places. Betting goes on largely; and that intermixture of the occupations of blackleg and politician, which is so common in the United States, is now to be seen in its perfection.

Franklin Pierce, Stephen A. Douglas, and James Buchanan are the candidates whose claims are understood to stand first in the order of precedence to be settled by the convention—the two former really reflecting but one interest or section of the party, the latter another. The first represents, with great accuracy, the party as it appears in the voice of its press, the acts and sentiments of its members of Congress, and the foreign and domestic policy of the executive government; and the nomination of Mr. Douglas, or the re-nomination of General Pierce would be the simple re-indorsement by the party of its declared principles and authentic history, and an appeal to the people for their ratification. The standing of Mr. Buchanan, on the other hand, is equivocal; and in this fact lies his strength — if strength he may be said to possess. Touching all the political questions now practical with the people of the United States, he is nowhere — represents nothing, and is to every intent and purpose, a negative. Nor is this the result of accident or want of opportunity to define his position. It is constitutional—inevitable. He would not be otherwise if he could, nor could he if he would. To occupy doctrinally a place certain, is totally foreign to his character. Those, therefore, who suppose that he stands, in regard to the policy of the government and party in the same place occupied by his adversaries, are mistaken; and those who believe that he stands in a different place are equally at fault. He stands nowhere. He never did stand anywhere.

There are, however, we are told, among the delegates, a large number, who are willing to suspend their principles for the sake of a successful election; and with such, Mr. Buchanan stands high as a candidate. The chance to give him, pending the canvass, either a Northern or Southern face, or both at once if it shall be deemed expedient, is too good to be thrown away. Having been about half a century in public life—one-half of which he spent in the bosom of the Federal, the other in that of the Democratic Party—this experienced and veteran camp-follower has learned, if nothing else, the benefits of non-committalism, and the art of holding his dish right side up, whatever may be the direction of the shower. . . .

It is not by any means impossible that a nominating portion of the delegates will deem it unsafe to face their principles by the choice of their recognized exponent, and will embrace the equivocation presented in the person of Mr. Buchanan, with the understanding—strengthened perhaps by private pledges— that after he is elected, he will *permit* his administration to be all that is desirable. A judicious distribution of such promises will enable him to combine the radical and conservative sections of the party North and South, while his great caution, extreme respectability, and Federal antecedents will secure to him a large body of the Whigs, the debris and rubbish of defunct organizations, and other fossil remains—the deposits of previous political revolutions. . . .

Recent events have in all probability tended to damage the prospects of the Pierce-Douglas faction in the convention. They have played the game of subserviency to the slave interest so strongly as to alarm many of their Southern friends, and there is great danger that their zeal for the cause has proved their destruction. Delegates from the South while approving what they have done, will dread the effects of the murder, robbery, and arson now taking place in Kansas under the patronage of the administration, upon the people of the North. Political gentlemen are ever ready to throw overboard those who have become obnoxious by their zeal, and it is reserved for this class to present the most shining examples of that exquisite variety of meanness—the sacrifice of their leaders because they have distinguished themselves in the leadership. This will account for an unexpected tendency towards Buchanan which is observable in several Southern delegations, which although it may not be sufficiently strong to secure his nomination, will defeat that of Pierce or Douglas, and render the selection of someone more neutral, if possible, than that gentleman, necessary to satisfy the demand for that nullity, both in principle and personality, usually required to harmonize a Democratic national convention.

Very Full and Fair Report

The Democratic Convention meets at Smith & Nixon's Hall this morning.[9] As there are not accommodations for a tithe of the multitudes that now swarm in the city, only delegates and reporters will be admitted. Numerous editions of the various papers of the city will be published during the session of the convention and the people thus posted as to its proceedings. We propose to give a very full and fair report of the performance— telling as nearly as possible the truth, the whole truth, and nothing but the truth, without reportorial comment or coloring. We occupy a wholly independent position, and have no disposition in this case to do otherwise than write history. So we commend the public to our columns, to observe the plain, unvarnished unfolding of the tale that is to be told.

General Appearance of Things

About ten o'clock crowds began to collect along Fourth Street between Main and Walnut, and many strangers looked in vain for the imposing front of the hall, the entrance being in appearance rather the reverse of conspicuous.[10] The representatives of the press were admitted to the hall by the rear entrance, the orders being very strict to permit no one to pass who was not provided with a ticket. A very considerable addition had been made to the stage for the accommodation of reporters, one hundred being provided for.

Pages were appointed—one for each state delegation. Seats were reserved specially for each delegation, and cards, with the names of the states prominently printed, were distributed. A little after eleven o'clock the delegates began to pour in, and it was a scene of much interest to observe the little boys holding up the names of the states, and the miscellaneous crowd, thus guided, resolving from chaos into order. . . .

Appearance of the Men

The representatives of the Democracy in convention assembled, are as a whole, good-looking men. The number of big rosy men is remarkable. The general appearance of the body of the delegates is decidedly superior to that of the House of Representatives. Among the other things, it is evident that the South has sent up its strong men to represent it on this occasion as usual. . . .

First Day – June 2

ORGANIZATION

Robert McLane, of Maryland, rose, and was received with cheers. He called the convention to order as chairman of the national committee. William A. Richardson, of Illinois, nominated Samuel Medary, of Ohio, as temporary chairman—adopted.

Benjamin F. Hallett, of Massachusetts, requested that the call for the convention be read. The reading was commenced by William H. English, of Indiana, member of Congress. At this moment it appeared that a large crowd had rushed past the guard at the door, and with wild cursing and shouts, lifting their fists and shaking their hats, they advanced into the hall. The sensation was intense. For a moment it seemed that there would be a general fight. The profanity was excessive. There were cries of "Shame," "Don't shoot," "Pitch in," and it was some five minutes before order was restored. . . .

Mr. Medary, of Ohio, was conducted to the chair and was enthusiastically received.

The chairman of the national convention handed the temporary chairman a list of delegates, and the credentials of two sets of delegates from New York (Hards and Softs,) and two from Mississippi. The committee had no preference. The delegations were required to select from the delegates the stipulated number allowed by the rules. The Mississippi delegation consented and made their choice, though eighty of them were now outside. This arrangement was not satisfactory to the New York delegations and they were now waiting (Hards and Softs) for admission to the hall. . . .

Mr. Albert Gallatin Brown, of Mississippi, offered a resolution authorizing the national convention to admit alternates and other delegates (not contestants) to seats in the gallery, and the vacant space in the rear of the hall. . . .

Mr. T. L. Harris, of Illinois, moved that a committee on credentials be appointed. Adopted. . . .

A Voice from the Illinois Delegation: In the name of the convention I invite the gentlemen from Missouri, not admitted on tickets, to retire. [Applause and furious hisses.]

George W. McCook, of Ohio, moved for a committee on permanent rules.

Ex-Senator Pettit, of Indiana: Order!

McCook: I mean temporary rules. . . .

A gallant gentleman moved that the front seats of the gallery all around, be reserved for the ladies, for, said he, without the ladies to look in upon us, we will be the most miserable men of the earth.

To this Honorable John Pettit, of Indiana, was opposed. He said:

"I am as much inclined to accommodate the ladies as any one, but I do think a resolution appropriating the entire gallery to their use, just now, would be as reasonable as that just proposed. The hall is now crowded to its utmost extent. The delegation from New York alone numbered 140, one-half of whom only were entitled to seats, and as soon as the committee on credentials would report, 70 of them would require places.

"On proper occasions, and in proper places, and then only, [Laughter], I would like to see the ladies accommodated; but in the present instance I shall move that the resolution (not the ladies) be laid on the table." [Great laughter.]

Disturbance in the Convention

The disturbance in the Democratic convention this morning was occasioned by the Benton delegation from Missouri, which the national committee had refused to recognise. They made an assault upon the doorkeepers and rushed into the main passage of the hall. About the time that they got fairly into the hall there was a vigorous display of pugilism, and several persons who opposed the Bentonites were knocked down, but amid cries of shame, the bold band of Missourians marched down the aisle and his friends got seats—shame, order, and other cries prevailed for a few minutes, and the convention then proceeded with its business. A favorable opportunity occurring, the leader of the Bentonites endeavored to address the chair, when the chairman refused to recognize him, and with his friends he bowed to the decision of the convention and retired. These were the points. The Bentonites were determined that the convention should take the responsibility of their rejection —that they would not be quietly ignored by the national committee—therefore did they make a forcible entry.

Appearance of Things Last Night – Rise in Douglas Stock

The indications last night were that Douglas stock had taken a rise. It had become evident during the day that the influential politicians assembled, the strong and accomplished wire-workers, the big *bluffers,* were for Douglas, and their chances to resist the outside pressure were, to say the least, good. If they could not nominate Douglas they would beat Buchanan, and bring out their own man. Such was the impression abroad, and in the evening the war between the Douglas and Buchanan factions waxed hot and bitter, and today it is expected to be fast and furious.

It was currently, and we think credibly, rumored at the Burnet House, last night, that a letter from Pierce had been received, requiring his friends to withdraw his name—not to allow his name to go before the convention at all. His strength will, of course, be thrown for Douglas.

The committee on permanent officers have selected for the very arduous and responsible position of chairman, General John E. Ward, of Georgia, who is understood to be a warm Pierce or Douglas man. This is an indication of the current of events which should be marked well. It certainly shows that the Pierce-Douglas men have the preponderance of strength in the committee of permanent officers. Then it is well known that the Douglas-Pierce men are the strongest element in the committee on credentials, before which the double sets of delegates from Missouri and New York have presented their case. It was stated last night that the committee had made their decision in the case of the Missourians, ruling out the Benton men, but we could not learn that this had absolutely been done.

But it certainly will be done, if it is not already a fact accomplished, for the reason that the Douglas men are strongest on the committee, and the Benton men are for Buchanan, and the anti-Benton men for Douglas. The rejection of the Benton men will be a heavy blow at Buchanan, and there will probably be a ferocious fight over it in convention. The Benton men say that if Douglas is nominated, Missouri cannot be carried for him, unless the Know Nothings go in with the nullifiers and go *en masse* for him. Old Bullion says: "Douglas can't carry a free state, sir—not a free state." If Buchanan is nominated, with or without the anti-Benton delegates, the Benton party will go for him—but it does not appear that they can go Douglas.

The committee on credentials have not decided on the case of the Hards and Softs of New York. Both sides of the case were presented before them last night, and they took time for consideration, proposing before making a decision to speak on the subject with their respective delegations, so as to know as nearly as possible the sense of the whole convention. In the Missouri case it is reported that they have been more hasty, but this is not positive. The bitterness of the Douglas men on the Benton delegates may be inferred from the remarks of William A. Richardson, of Illinois, who is little Dug's right bower, on the forcible entry into the hall of the Bentonians. He was very emphatic in characterizing their proceedings as an insult to the convention, and in affirming that the convention should protect itself. The feeling of the convention may be seen in the fact that Richardson's remarks were received with hearty approbation, while the Missourians were called to order, and so hissed and hooted at that they were not heard at all.

There was one movement of the South which was defeated— that was the proposition to admit masses of alternate delegates from Mississippi, and other Southern states to the vacant seats in the hall. This was defeated by the resolute adroitness of some Northwestern men. Looking carefully at all the shadows of events past and to come we think that Douglas is looming up.

Young Men's Democratic Meeting

Another immense concourse of the Democracy assembled at Greenwood Hall, last night, for the purpose of hearing addresses from some of the leading Democrats of the Union. The meeting was first addressed by Mr. W. D. Bishop, of Connecticut, who was followed by Charles Carrigan, of Philadelphia, Honorable Samuel Smith, of Tennessee, Judge S. S. Brown, of New York, and Captain Isaiah Rynders, of New York City. The speeches were all characterized more or less by a degree of eloquence, and those of Messrs. Bishop and Carrigan were masterly efforts.

While Judge Brown was speaking he mentioned the names of the most prominent candidates for the presidential chair. The name of Pierce being passed over in silence—when he spoke of Douglas a hearty cheer resounded through the hall, but when the name of Buchanan was mentioned the demonstrations of approbation were so great that he was unable to proceed for several minutes. The speeches were all of a "Union saving" character, each orator proclaiming in turn that the salvation of the Union was alone with the Democratic Party.

The principal tenor of Captain Rynders' remarks was a description of his attack on a Free Soil convention, a few years since. He said the fight was a free one; that he made it himself, and that whenever he did make a fight he was sure to come out first-best. "When the fight was over," said Captain R., "there was black wool and white wool enough lying about to make mattresses enough for all the niggers in South Carolina!"

Second Day – June 3

ORGANIZATION

The convention was called to order by the chairman, Colonel Samuel Medary, at ten minutes past 10 A.M.[11] Mr. John L. Dawson, of Pennsylvania, from the committee on permanent officers, reported: President, John E. Ward, of Georgia.

The committee on permanent officers reported that it recommended the rules and regulations adopted by the national Democratic convention in 1852, be adopted by this convention for their government. . . .

John E. Ward, president elect, on being conducted to the chair, addressed the convention as follows:

Gentlemen of the Convention: The summons to preside over your deliberations is as unexpected as it is grateful to me. The distinguished gentleman who yesterday presided here, is a connecting link between the political past and present. He carried us back to that period when this same Democratic Party assembled to give her commission to her favorite son, [cheers for Andrew Jackson] to go forth and battle with that noble and gallant party which *then* contested with us for the suffrages of the American people. *That* party with its issues has passed away; its leaders, one by one, have stolen away to their silent resting places, ripe in years, ripe in honors. . . . But others of the old leaders of that party are with us today [applause] in our deliberations, and ready to battle with us for the Constitution and the Union.

Why? Why then, gentlemen of the convention, with this great party—great in principles, venerable in age, environed with difficulties, surrounded with dangers as never before, should we not determine at the outset to act in entire concert, with unity of purpose?

Our country is convulsed by factions; one faction, recreant to the Constitution, would build a wall around the land, and give to the exiles of other lands no entrance, no asylum, but on conditions of serfdom. The emigrant must bow before the same altar, his enthusiasm must be kindled at the same shrine as theirs; he must approach the Throne of Grace through the forms prescribed by them—if nay, upon his conscience, there is for him no America.

That other faction, more dangerous only because more numerous, with *liberty* on their tongues, but *treason* festering in their hearts, [tumultuous cheering in front] with treason in their hearts, go forth against our Union—and, gentlemen, they hope that Union may dissolve—they would bury in a common ruin all our National Past and its Future! Each of these factions, by itself contemptible, becomes formidable, as it betrays tendencies to unite against that party that yields nothing, advances not into the untried, admits of no affiliations. [General applause]

Here are assembled the representative delegates of that party; we are here from the Pacific on the West, the lakes on the North, the Atlantic on the East, and from the farthest South. We have come up to present a platform and a STANDARD BEARER against these factions. [Manifestations of approbation]

Let us "go at them" [cheers] as a band of brothers; we will lay on the altar of a common country the minor dissents, the passions, the interests, and, above all, private friendships. We will be guided by our chart of principles, will be animated by a higher, purer love of country, in which the love of friends and the easier sacrificed love of self shall be lost in the emulation to preserve the Constitution. . . .

James Bayard of Delaware, from the committee on credentials, reported. The point of this was that the Benton delegation was ruled out, which announcement was received with faint applause. . . .

Senator Albert Gallatin Brown, of Mississippi, offered two resolutions declaring the galleries vacant and empowering the committee on arrangements to issue tickets to the delegates from states and territories; tickets pro-rate to be given National Democrats in attendance for seats in the gallery. . . .

Mr. Benjamin F. Hallett, of Massachusetts, said that as chairman of the committee on resolutions, he would state that the committee would be prepared to report, the first thing in the morning. And he suggested that the platform be made the special order for ten o'clock in the morning. There would be printed copies of the platform ready for delegates and reporters, when it was reported.

The motion to adjourn until ten o'clock A.M., June 4th, was then renewed and carried, and the convention adjourned. . . .

*   *   *

Facts and Fancies Afloat

The crowd in the office of the Burnet House was not so large and turbulent last night, as for some evenings previous. The Buchanan men said very confidently, when asked about the prospects of their man, "Oh! It's all fixed. Buchanan will be nominated, sure as the world." On the other hand the Douglas men said warmly when interrogated in the same style: "Buchanan can never be nominated in the world." The Ohio delegation was polled, informally of course, yesterday; and the result was, 14 votes for Buchanan and 9 for Douglas. The New England delegations are counted on as almost unanimously for Buchanan after a few ballots. It is said that the Louisiana delegation held a caucus yesterday, and overruling Pierre Soule, concluded that they might go for Buchanan.

The Douglas men say that there are 107 votes in the convention that cannot, under any circumstances, be obtained for Buchanan. If this is so he cannot be nominated under the two-third rule now adopted. This rule requires in this case 197 votes to nominate, and we do not see at all clearly where more than 160 Buchanan votes can be found.

The Illinois delegation held a long private caucus last night, and the conjecture was that they were deliberating how best to withdraw Little Dug without damaging him. William A. Richardson, of Illinois, and John C. Breckinridge, of Kentucky, had an anxious talk. We presume there is little doubt that the withdrawal of Douglas was under consideration. But the question is, whether if he be withdrawn, his supporters will nominate Buchanan with a rush and at one plunge, or will put up another man—Lewis Cass, of Michigan, or Thomas Jefferson Rusk, of Texas, for instance. The betting men about town are making extravagant offers to back Buchanan with their cash.

A great effort was made last week in behalf of Howell Cobb, of Georgia, for Vice-President. But the fact that a Georgian was selected to preside over the convention, and that the Georgia platform is the basis of the one to be adopted, would indicate that Mr. Cobb was out of the ring. It would not do to shower all the honors upon Georgia. General John A. Quitman is much talked of for the vice presidency. If Buchanan is nominated for President, undoubtedly a Southern man will be selected for Vice-President.

There was a rumor, strongly endorsed, yesterday afternoon, that the Buchanan men were sure of obtaining a majority of the votes in the convention, and that if it appeared impossible to obtain two-thirds, they would move that Buchanan be declared the nominee, and in case they were defeated in this, would withdraw from the convention, repudiate its proceedings, issue an address to the Democracy, and declare Buchanan the candidate. If the fight waxes hot, and passions are excited to the uttermost, it is not improbable that this action will be taken, as the Buchananiers are opposed, in the most intense degree, to Pierce or Douglas, or any man of their manufacture.

The controversy of the New York delegations before the committee on credentials occupied that committee yesterday and last night. The arguments on both sides were elaborate and able, and not acrimonious. At a late hour last night, the committee had not arrived at any definite determination. The fight between the Hards and Softs involves the whole hideous complication of New York politics, about which there is as great confusion of tongues as occurred in the vicinity of the tower of Babel. It is not probable that the committee will take the responsibility of indorsing in full, either faction as the old regular, simon pure, original "Old Dr. Jacob Townsend"[12] Democracy, or of stamping it the spurious article. It is probable that both will be admitted to seats, or both excluded. It would be so palpable an act of partiality to show favoritism to either, that we presume the responsibility of making a decision one way or the other, will be evaded. Judge Greene C. Bronson and

D. L. Seymour presented the case of the Hards, and Governor
Horatio Seymour and L. B. Shepard for the Softs. Some of the
Southerners said that both sets of delegates were excellent fellows, and they really couldn't see what was so persistently
quarrelled about. . . .

There was to those who looked upon the proceedings of the
Democratic convention yesterday, or who attentively read the
reports thereof, something strange in the quiet, unanimous,
matter-of-course manner in which the famous two-third rule
was adopted, and the Benton delegation from Missouri ruled
out.[13] Not a voice was lifted in opposition to these highly important movements. The question occurred: were the Buchanan
men about to surrender without a struggle? Or had they suffi-
cient assurance of strength to warrant them in letting these
preliminary matters slide smoothly? Public opinion held that
the whole thing was cut and dried for Buchanan, who would
stand on an ultra Southern platform. This is the old story—a
Northern man with Southern principles—a man from the North
and a platform from the South. JAMES BUCHANAN ON THE
GEORGIA PLATFORM was the word yesterday afternoon.
The Georgia resolutions are ultra Southern, going in for the
Nebraska Bill, and if our impression is correct, it is for UNION
conditional upon the CONSTITUTIONAL RIGHT of slave-
holders to enjoy the peculiar privileges attending to the peculiar
institution, in all the territories. That these Georgia resolutions
are the foundation and compose the principal portion of the
platform that will be presented today by Mr. Benjamin Hallet,
we are positively and reliably informed. The Benton men,
though turned out of the convention, avow their determination
to support Buchanan if he should be the nominee, reserving to
themselves the privilege of "splitting on the platform."

Third Day – June 4

PLATFORM

The convention was called to order at 10 o'clock by the
chairman, with whom Richardson of Illinois, held an earnest

conference, and after some minutes' confusion, Mr. James A. Stewart, of Maryland, called for the regular order of business.[14]

Mr. Hallet of Massachusetts then reported the following platform:

Resolved, That the American Democracy place their trust in the intelligence, the patriotism, and the discriminating justice of the American people.

Resolved, That we regard this as a distinctive feature of our political creed, which we are proud to maintain before the world, as the great moral element in a form of government springing from and upheld by the popular will; and we contrast it with the creed and practice of Federalism, under whatever name or form, which seeks to palsy the will of the constituent, and which conceives no imposture too monstrous for the popular credulity.

Resolved, therefore, That, entertaining these views, the Democratic party of this Union, through their delegates assembled in a general convention, coming together in a spirit of concord, of devotion to the doctrines and faith of a free representative government, and appealing to their fellow-citizens for the rectitude of their intentions, renew and reassert before the American people, the declarations of principles avowed by them when, on former occasions, in general convention, they have presented their candidates for the popular suffrages.

1. That the federal government is one of limited power, derived solely from the Constitution. . . .

2. That the Constitution does not confer upon the general government the power to commence and carry on a general system of internal improvements.

3. That the Constitution does not confer authority upon the federal government, directly or indirectly, to assume the debts of the several states, contracted for local and internal improvements. . . .

4. That justice and sound policy forbid the federal government to foster one branch of industry to the detriment of any other, or to cherish the interests of one portion to the injury of another portion of our common country; that every citizen and every section of the country has a right to demand and insist upon an equality of rights and privileges, and to complete and ample protection of persons and property from violence or foreign aggression.

5. That it is the duty of every branch of the government to enforce and practice the most rigid economy. . . .

6. That the proceeds of the public lands ought to be sacredly applied to the national objects specified in the Constitution; and that we are opposed to any law for the distribution of such proceeds among the states, as alike inexpedient in policy and repugnant to the Constitution.

7. That Congress has no power to charter a national bank; that we believe such an institution one of deadly hostility to the best interests of the country, dangerous to our republican institutions and the liberties of the people, and calculated to place the business of the country within the control of a concentrated money power, and above the laws and the will of the people. . . .

10. That the liberal principles embodied by Jefferson in the Declaration of Independence, and sanctioned in the Constitution, which makes ours the land of liberty, and the asylum of the oppressed of every nation, have ever been cardinal principles in the Democratic faith, and every attempt to abridge the privilege of becoming citizens and the owners of soil among us, ought to be resisted with the same spirit which swept the alien and sedition laws from our statute books.

And WHEREAS, Since the foregoing declaration was uniformly adopted by our predecessors in national conventions, an adverse political and religious test has been secretly organized by a party claiming to be exclusively American, it is proper that the American Democracy should clearly define its relations thereto, and declare its determined opposition to all secret political societies, by whatever name they may be called.

Resolved, That the foundation of this union of states having been laid in, and its prosperity, and pre-eminent example in free government built upon entire freedom in matters of religious concernment, and no respect of person in regard to rank or place of birth; no party can justly be deemed national, constitutional, or in accordance with American principles, which bases its exclusive organization upon religious opinions and accidental birthplace. And hence a political crusade in the nineteenth century, and in the United States of America, against Catholics and foreign-born, is neither justified by the past history or the future prospects of the country, nor in unison with the spirit of toleration enlarged freedom which peculiarly distinguishes the American system of popular government.

Resolved, That we reiterate, with renewed energy of purpose, the well-considered declarations of former conventions upon the sectional issue of domestic slavery, and concerning the reserved rights of the states:

1. That Congress has no power, under the Constitution, to interfere with or control the domestic institutions of the several states, and that such states are the sole and proper judges of everything appertaining to their own affairs, not prohibited by the Constitution; that all efforts of the Abolitionists or others, made to induce Congress to interfere with questions of slavery, or to take incipient steps in relation thereto, are calculated to lead to the most alarming and dangerous consequences; and that all such efforts have an inevitable tendency to diminish the happiness of the people, and endanger the stability and permanency of the Union, and ought not to be countenanced by any friend of our political institutions.

2. That the foregoing proposition covers, and was intended to embrace, the whole subject of slavery agitation in Congress; and therefore, the Democratic party of the Union, standing on this national platform, will abide by and adhere to a faithful execution of the acts known as the compromise measures, settled by the Congress of 1850; "the act for reclaiming fugitives from service or labor," included; which act being designed to carry out an express provision of the Constitution, cannot, with fidelity thereto, be repealed, or so changed as to destroy or impair its efficiency.

3. That the Democratic party will resist all attempts at renewing, in Congress or out of it, the agitation of the slavery question under whatever shape or color the attempt may be made. . . .

And that we may more distinctly meet the issue on which a sectional party, subsisting exclusively on slavery agitation, now relies to test the fidelity of the people, North and South, to the Constitution and the Union:

1. Resolved, That claiming fellowship with, and desiring the co-operation of all who regard the preservation of the Union under the Constitution as the paramount issue—and repudiating all sectional parties and platforms concerning domestic slavery, which seek to embroil the states and incite to treason and armed resistance to law in the territories; and whose avowed purposes, if consummated, must end in civil war and disunion—the American Democracy recognize and adopt the principles contained in the organic laws establishing the territories of Kansas and Nebraska as embodying the only sound and safe solution of the "slavery question" upon which the great national idea of the people of this whole country can repose in its determined conservatism of the Union—NON-INTERFERENCE BY CONGRESS WITH SLAVERY IN THE TERRITORIES OR IN THE DISTRICT OF COLUMBIA. . . .

Resolved, That we recognize the right of the people of all the territories, including Kansas and Nebraska, acting through the legally and fairly expressed will of a majority of actual residents, and whenever the number of their inhabitants justifies it, to form a Constitution, with or without domestic slavery, and be admitted into the Union upon terms of perfect equality with the other states.

Resolved, finally, That in view of the condition of popular institutions in the Old World (and the dangerous tendencies of sectional agitation, combined with the attempt to enforce civil and religious disabilities against the rights of acquiring and enjoying citizenship, in our own land) a high and sacred duty is devolved with increased responsibility upon the Democratic party of this country, as the party of the Union, to uphold and maintain the rights of every State, and thereby the Union of the States; and to sustain and advance among us Constitutional liberty, by continuing to resist all monopolies and exclusive legislation for the benefit of the few at the expense of the many, and by a vigilant and constant adherence to those principles and compromises of the Constitution, which are broad enough and strong enough to embrace and uphold the Union as it was, the Union as it is, and the Union as it shall be, in the full expansion of the energies and capacity of this great and progressive people:

1. Resolved, That there are questions connected with the foreign policy of this country, which are inferior to no domestic question whatever. The time has come for the people of the United States to declare themselves in favor of free seas and progressive free trade throughout the world, and, by solemn manifestations, to place their moral influence at the side of their successful example.

2. Resolved, . . . that we should hold as sacred the principles involved in the Monroe Doctrine. . . .

4. Resolved, . . . the people of the United States cannot but sympathize with the efforts which are being made by the people of Central America to regenerate that portion of the continent which covers the passage across the interoceanic isthmus.

5. *Resolved,* That the Democratic party will expect of the next administration that every proper effort be made to insure our ascendancy in the Gulf of Mexico, and to maintain a permanent protection to the great outlets through which are emptied into its waters the products raised out of the soil, and the commodities created by the industry of the people of our western valleys, and of the Union at large.

Resolved, That the Democratic party recognizes the great importance in political and commercial point of view, of a safe and speedy communication by military and postal roads, through our own territory, between the Atlantic and Pacific Coasts of this Union, and that it is the duty of the federal government to exercise promptly all its Constitutional power for the attainment of that object.

Mr. Hallett stated that that portion of the platform having reference to the Nebraska Bill had been adopted with entire unanimity—each member from every state had voted for it heartily. The resolution having reference to the foreign policy of the government, he was instructed to say, had not been adopted unanimously, though by a large majority. There was also some difference of opinion on the Pacific Railroad clause.

How the Platform Was Received

The announcement of the unanimity in favor of the Nebraska Bill was received with applause. The anti-Know Nothing clauses were heard with fierce and noisy approbation. The slavery clauses were given double rounds of stamping and cheers. The New England delegates were generally quiet when the Fugitive Slave resolutions were read. The direct reference to the Kansas-Nebraska Bill was heard with tremendous and long continued demonstrations of approval, which were so persistent that it had finally rather an artificial and forced sound.

Without any intention to be invidious, we must remark that the intensity of the enthusiasm, the flinging up of hats and waving of handkerchiefs, did not appear to be genuinely thorough and spontaneous.

The reference to the foreign policy—free seas, free trade, and the Monroe Doctrine—was not welcomed with such enormous demonstrations as were the slavery points. The approbation for the filibuster clauses—Central America and Cuba—was weak. The Pacific Railroad applause was slight. . . .

The vote on all of the report relating to the domestic policy of the Union was now taken by states, with the following result: For the platform, 139; against, none. So the platform, so far as relating to slavery and the whole domestic policy of the country, was adopted by a unanimous vote.

The North Carolina, the Mississippi and the Virginia delegations now entered the hall and, after some little hesitation, severally announced the entire votes of their respective states for the platform, which was carried by 296 for—to none against. Before casting the vote of Virginia, Mr. Muscoe R. H. Garnett had insisted with intense earnestness that his delegation should be allowed to pause before committing the Old Dominion to a policy she had forever opposed. Virginia was only ready to vote in favor of the "domestic policy" portion of the report.

Attempts to Adjourn

Charles A. Wickliffe, of Kentucky, rose to beg the convention to give himself and others time to read over the balance of the report in the cool air with leisure, to see what it really was. . . .

Finally, after half a dozen ineffectual motions for a recess, a motion to adjourn till 2 P.M. carried.

Afternoon Session

At the demand of a delegate, the convention was called to order at twenty minutes past two, by the chairman.

During the recess, some enterprising individual, who had made his way between the ceiling and the roof, managed to get his leg into the hall, by inserting it through the ceiling, to the sudden dislodgment of a large quantity of lath and plastering. . . .

The first resolution having reference to foreign policy, was then put and voted upon by states. The vote resulted 211 aye, to 49 no. The negative votes were from Kentucky, Mississippi, Connecticut, and Delaware. This resolution is now one that goes in for "free seas and progressive free trade throughout the world."

The second resolution was then before the convention, and

on a vote by states the result was 239 ayes to 23 noes. The point of this resolution is, that "we should hold as sacred the principles involved in the Monroe Doctrine." The negative votes were from Rhode Island, Delaware, and Georgia.

Wickliffe, of Kentucky, asked leave to change from the negative to the affirmative, the vote of that state on the first resolution. Leave granted.

The next resolution, the one relating to the "free communication between the Atlantic and Pacific Oceans," through Central America, was taken up, and the vote by states resulted as follows . . . : 211 yeas, 49 nays.

The resolution relating to sympathy with the efforts made by the people of Central America (Walker)[15] was passed on a vote by states . . . , 209 yeas, 40 nays.

The resolution recommending the establishment of a post road, etc., across the continent was then taken up. . . .

On the motion to lay on the table, the resolution in favor of a post road to the Pacific, the vote by states was demanded, and resulted as follows . . . : 142 yeas, 102 nays.

So the post road does not go into the platform. . . .

Next came up the Gulf of Mexico resolution, squinting toward Cuba . . .: 229 yeas, 30 nays.

Judge James W. Borden, of Indiana, moved . . . that a committee of one from each state, to be selected by the delegates thereof, be appointed to report the names of persons to constitute the Democratic national committee, and the mode of constituting and calling the next Democratic convention. Adopted. . . .

A delegate enquired when it was likely the committee on credentials would report.

John Pettit of Indiana: Sir, time enough has passed since Monday at noon, in waiting for New York to settle her intestine quarrels. I do now move that the convention proceed to the nomination of a candidate for the presidency. [Cheers]

Willard Saulsbury of Delaware: We oppose that; give us time for cool reflection—tomorrow will be soon enough to act upon so great a question. . . .

On motion by a delegate from Kentucky, the convention agreed to adjourn till nine o'clock tomorrow morning, (Thursday) with the understanding that the New York question should then be settled, and that the convention would immediately thereafter proceed to nominate a candidate for the presidency.

*   *   *

Personal Appearance of Prominent Men

The chairman, John E. Ward, of Georgia, is a tall gentleman whose figure would by an artist be pronounced good.[16] He is dressed in dark clothes, and his complexion is swarthy, his voice shrill and usually very distinct; but it gives out, cracks, at a high pitch. His manner is ordinarily very decisive, and he inclines to be rigid in the enforcement of the rules. Many knotty parliamentary points are tied and tangled for his solution, and he occasionally defers much to members of Congress on the floor—but is a very efficient presiding officer. Harry Hibbard, of New Hampshire, seems to be his parliamentary adviser. Hibbard has a seat near the stage, on the speaker's left, and gives the votes of New Hampshire. He is tall and slender, wears glasses and is decidedly intellectual in appearance, his forehead being high and fair, his cheeks lean and his lips, though not thin, tightly compressed. His voice is strong and full of emphasis. He has served eight years in the House of Representatives, and lost his seat in consequence of his vote for the Nebraska bill. He is a fast friend of Frank Pierce, and is the organ of his corner of the hall.

Under the gallery next the eastern aisle, (to the left of the chairman) is Benjamin F. Butler, of Massachusetts, a short, nervous man, with a bald head, and slight sandy moustache. About the back of his head and above his ears are a few dry looking foxy hairs, which seem to have been parched by the excessive heat of his brain. He is intense and inflammable as a Chinese cracker, and makes his points with a sharp ferocity of utterance almost startling. His voice is not strong, but keen and piercing, and yet occasionally is husky with the vehemence of passion, which seems ready to blaze from him in dire combustion.

Close to this peculiar personage is Benjamin F. Hallet, who reported the platform—the distinguished gentleman who also reported a famous set of resolutions to a Democratic Massachusetts convention, two or three years ago, in which he said that the Democracy of that state were in favor of "FREEDOM ALL OVER GOD'S HERITAGE," which phrase is now the motto of the Massachusetts Republicans, and is emblazoned on their big banner in Boston. He is a short, heavy, rather peaceable looking gentleman, whose general appearance suggests many good dinners and considerable intellectual vigor. He read the platform excellently well.

Near the eastern aisle and within a few seats of the front—on the western side of the aisle—sits John C. Breckinridge, the impersonation of Democratic Kentucky chivalry, who won a high position in the last Congress, and declined to be a candidate for re-election. He is a tall and gracefully formed young man, with delicate features, and would be singularly handsome if his profile line was more prominent. Looking at him sideways, his forehead, nose and chin, are nearly in straight line. But his eye beams with intelligence, his nose is handsome in outline, and the habitual compression of his lips indicates a resolute will. On the whole there is a poetic glimmer about him. And that there is something of this in his character, the fact that he has purchased an island in Lake Superior for a summer home, would indicate. His manner in speaking is proud, defiant, and full of passion, tempered by educated discretion.

In the Kentucky delegation, near the front is Charles A. Wickliffe, Esq., who looks to perfection the old Kentucky aristocrat. The only thing Democratic that can be seen about him is the handkerchief with which he wipes the perspiration from his brow, and which appears to be a red and white cotton article. His dress is rich, and has the cut and fit characteristic of a fine old Kentucky gentleman. His countenance is stern, and his bearing that which should be anticipated of grave old gentlemen of high character in the United States Senate or British House of Lords. It would not require any shrewdness of observation to discover that he is the autocrat of a plantation. He is large in frame and fleshy, his face much wrinkled, and his hair nearly all gone. His voice is good, but he is not calculated to be a leader in a Democratic convention. The "noise and confusion" perplexes, annoys him. He is not accustomed to be interrupted, and badgered on all sides.

Richard K. Meade, of Virginia, a fine specimen of the old school Old Dominion gentleman, is sitting near the central aisle, in the eastern division of seats, and some twenty chairs from the chairman. He is large, handsome, dressed richly, and is courtly in style, and says that which he has to say well, but not with overwhelming power. He, too, is oppressed with the devilish din around him, and there is a paucity of bright sandy hair on his round and placid head. Honorable Fayette McMullen, of Virginia, is a large man, who speaks hurriedly, and with a singular flutter in the large volume of sound which he emits, and who does not often happen to hit the nail on the head in his remarks. There is evidently a large amount of self-complacency buttoned away snugly under his spacious yellow vest.

Peleg C. Child, of Connecticut, sitting in the southeastern part of the hall, is a charming old fellow. Good humor and good will to man have doubtless glistened in his broad face for more than three-score years, and the wrinkles worn there have been by the flow of the milk of human kindness. But whenever he rises to speak, it seems to be a matter of conjecture whether some full-fed, large-hearted, old style Methodist preacher has not strayed down from Indianapolis, and got into the *convention* instead of into the *conference.* There is a twang, very like that to which we are accustomed from the Methodist pulpit, in his utterances; and on Tuesday he produced quite a sensation in the convention by calling on delegates to "give their experience." His voice is full, and has a ponderous gurgle, and rolls about the hall with triumphant approbation of itself and the sentiments it delivers, in every tone, and swells up like the mellow blast of a keel-boatman's horn (of the kind of which General William O. Butler sung)[17] amid the storm of plaudits sure to come.

To the right of the chairman, (near the west central aisle,) and well back, may be seen that world-wide celebrity, Pierre Soule. He would probably weigh about one hundred and eighty pounds and is very slightly round-shouldered, but his limbs are straight and handsome. His white vest curves comfortably outward, showing a moderate appreciation in the past of good things to eat, and that good digestion has waited on appetite. The expression of his face is *quite French,* but this in a Napoleonic sense. His lower jaw is firm as iron, a Frenchman's vague, polite smile, lingers and plays on his lip, and he has a beaming eye, and a forehead not huge at all, but rounded out, and seamed and paled with thought, and the passion of many a war within the brain of which it is the index, and the wear and tear of many a rude shock, amid the contentions of the world. As he turns his head, his eye gleams with a flash that might well excite apprehensions in a foe. Therein shines the fire of the filibuster, of the man who shot the French minister at the court of Madrid,[18] and incurred the bitter personal enmity of the French emperor and empress, which Paris letter-writers say he still enjoys. His once black and heavy hair, now thin and slightly silvered, is brushed back straight and close to the scalp, revealing completely the fine outlines of his head. As yet he has not spoken a word in convention.

On the extreme right of the speaker, near one of the pillars of the gallery, John Pettit, of Indiana, (who was labelled for time and eternity by Colonel Thomas Hart Benton)[19] looms up at frequent intervals, short but thick, brief yet enormous—looking like a giant *squeezed down* in Gabriel Ravel's magic man press. When he rises, he presents a broad patch of bald head, a queerly arranged big fat face, a vast belly, and legs like those of an elephant. His voice seems to roll up from some boundless and thunderous region, and reverberates solemnly above the tumult like the booming of a monstrous bull frog amid a concert of frogs of far inferior wind privileges. Imagine a bull frog played upon by a steam whistle, and you have it. And that which he says is to the point, and potent too. His thunder is not an empty sound, but roars with veritable significance.

One of the most active men in the hall is William A. Richardson, of Illinois, a tall, firmly built, coarse featured man, who stoops slightly, and with anxious inflinching gaze, regards every movement of the slightest importance. He is the right bower of Douglas, was the champion of the Nebraska bill in the House, yet was re-elected, and was the regular Democratic candidate for the speaker of the House last winter. There is evidently a large amount of that excellent quality which we call *humanity* in the man, and he is working for Douglas here with the most intense devotion. But his face does not shine with the interior inspiration of victory. His smiles are only skin deep, and there is something of sorrow, and weariness with unrequited toil, in every deep line that seams his face, out of which his great Roman nose stands like a promontory defying sea and sky with all their storms. Briefly said, he looks like pictures of Black Hawk, only his costume is that of civilization. Great attention is paid to whatever he says, and when he goes into a fight he generally fixes it his own way. His voice is ample, yet far from melodious, and its modulation shows the Sucker stump speaker unmistakably, being a queer compound of the *b'hoyish* and the back woods style of utterance, with a gloss of that which is learned beneath the dome of the House of Representatives in our national capitol.

Massachusetts in the Pillory

When the president called for the vote of Massachusetts, in the convention yesterday, on the Kansas-Nebraska platform, reported by Mr. "Gods-Heritage" Hallet, thirteen men rose up, two with some alacrity, the others more painfully. Among the "solid men of Boston," whose smile of approval, as spokesman Butler cried "unanimously *aye*," was ghastlier than that of their New England fellows along the east wall, were Messrs. Whitting Griswold, Isaac Davis, and James H. Whitney. We believe that each of these pilloried individuals once honored themselves and their state by voting for Charles Sumner for United States Senator.

Fourth Day – June 5

Scenes in the Convention – Nominations – Galleries
First Ballot – Decline of Pierce Strength

There were frequently scenes in the convention, on yesterday, full of exciting interest.[20] The announcement that the convention would proceed to ballot for a candidate, was made in a shrill voice, amid "noise and confusion" that would have made Cass crazy. The first announcement of a candidate was by Richard K. Meade, of Virginia, who named James Buchanan, which was followed by a roar of applause. Harry Hibbard named Pierce, and was also applauded. Richardson arose, but Colonel Samuel W. Inge, of California, was ahead of him, and, to the astonishment of many persons, named Lewis Cass, who was honored with a rattle of surprise rather than approving animation. Meade, Hibbard, and Inge, each indulged in a brief flourish of trumpets, but William A. Richardson simply said: *"I nominate Stephen A. Douglas, of Illinois."* This had the ring of the true manly metal, and was so recognized. There was something like grandeur in the rigid simplicity of the nomination.

A dense multitude now gazed down from the galleries, a mass of men filled the space behind the seats, under the gallery near the front door, and crowds of super-numeraries gathered thick among the sweltering reporters and officers on the stage. Most of the delegations were in anxious, confused consultation; the aisles were filled by the busy throngs; and adventurous spectators peered in at the high round windows. The air was hot, and only moved by the flutter of a thousand fans—while many who had assiduously fanned themselves before, now forgot the oppressiveness of the atmosphere in the more fierce inner heat of the excitement; and their palm leaves were still, while the perspiration glistened on their faces, undimmed by handkerchiefs. The secretary arose to call the states, a hundred reporters grasped their newly sharpened pencils, ready to be the historians of the events whose shadows were impending; and across the upper northwestern corner of the hall were two bright copper wires, through which the continent listened.

Maine was first called, and the announcement by her spokesman was five votes for Buchanan and three for Pierce. Then Hibbard responded for New Hampshire: "Five votes for Franklin Pierce," as if he intended to vote that way until doomsday. The Massachusetts delegation was divided, Butler giving their vote with sharp, quick tones, causing a jerking of heads in his direction. Connecticut came in for Buchanan, and there were cheers and hisses. The chairman smote the table violently with his hammer, and looked daggers. Gentlemen had been earnestly requested to refrain from all manifestations of applause, and there were threats of clearing the galleries. Then came New York, and the Softs gave eighteen votes for Pierce, and the Hards, through their stern and white-haired leader, Samuel Beardsley, the veteran of a long war of brotherly hate, gave seventeen votes for Buchanan. In spite of the vehement effort of the chair, and numerous calls to order, there was a burst of applause followed by a storm of shrill hisses; now New Jersey gave her whole vote for Buchanan, and next Pennsylvania resonantly called, rolled in twenty-seven votes for her "favorite son," and again applause and hisses rang through the hall; but the feeling was growing too strong for such expression. Maryland went "six for Buchanan, three for Pierce," and Delaware three for Buchanan, and then old Virginia gave her whole vote with emphasis for Buchanan and heightened the sensation greatly. Now come a string of the cotton states for Pierce, but Louisiana broke the charm of association by wheeling into the Buchanan line, leaving her Southern sisters sorrowing. Now "Ohio," the secretary called in a big, mellow rolling voice, but she "passed," and after a season of agonizing consultation gave her vote in fractions, spoiling the effect, but the weight of her strength was for Buchanan. Wickliffe answered for Kentucky, but was bothered by the division of her vote, not getting it right until the third trial, when he was greeted by a laugh and took his seat, his face solemn and wrathful as a lurid thunder cloud. His anger was almost too big for him, and it seemed doubtful whether he would suffocate it, or it him, but he at length conquered. Tennessee went for Pierce, but this was known to be an empty compliment only. Indiana was answered for by a rosy old gentleman who with a smile of exultation, and in a rich, swelling, jubilant voice said "thirteen for Buchanan." Illinois went solid for her own "little Dug," and Missouri followed, and through all the ballots did not falter. Texas from the frontier Southwest, spoke for Pierce, then Wisconsin, young but great, having to the world's eye only just emerged from the cold mists of the far Northwest, divided her vote between Buchanan and Douglas, and next distant magic, magnificent California, sent up her voice solitary and alone through sheer vexation, for Cass. The votes were read over for verification, there was a profound silence, and the hum of conversation was faint, while the secretaries footed up the figures. [Buchanan, 135½; Pierce, 122½; Douglas, 33; and Cass, 5.] The announcement of the first ballot was made, there was a slight tumult as the number of votes cast for each candidate was proclaimed, the chair stated quickly that no nomination had been effected, the secretary began to call the states again, and at intervals, the click of the telegraph could be heard in the corner, telling, from Bangor to New Orleans, Chicago to Charleston, and from St. Louis to Boston, all our towns and cities, of the first ballot.

There were no exciting changes during the first five ballots, and the only episode worthy of note was the fall of one of the "Star Spangled Banners" which decorated the stage, and that that little incident diversified the performance directly after the announcement of a vote for Pierce. Whether it be ominous or not, it is certain that "the flag of our country" for a minute was "trailing in the dust." On the sixth ballot Tennessee went over to Buchanan, causing a fierce excitement, which broke out in mingled hisses and stamping, and was with difficulty checked by the chair. But on the next trial Tennessee took another lurch, casting her vote for Douglas, and this she continued to do until adjournment.

As the vote for Pierce sunk, which it did on every ballot, the face of Hibbard of New Hampshire waxed solemn, and finally took a fixed expression of sad, despairing determination. Delegates gathered around and whispered to him, seemingly endeavoring to persuade him to withdraw poor Frank; but his features never relaxed, and at every call for New Hampshire he gave her vote for the president in full stern tones, and twice voted against adjournment. At length he gave the vote of his state to adjourn, and this was recognized by friend and foe as a signal of distress. The voting was singularly rapid. The secretary would give the result of a ballot, and in the same instant the chair would order the vote by states again; and the secretary would cry out "Maine" with the second breath after that in which he had told the story of the preceding vote. The telegraph was in constant operation, messenger boys were hurrying to and fro, delegates could be heard making pathetic appeals to each other's generosity, Democracy, and patriotism; and tones of reproach, and of approval, of anger and of satisfaction, mingled in a deep, anxious murmur just drowning the rustling of the fans. In one of the west windows appeared the head and hands of a man, with an umbrella to shield him from the sun and showers which alternated, and he was busily employed in keeping tally in a note book, and calling out the figures to the merchants who were on the watch at the back windows of their exchange. Notwithstanding the official proclamation of peace between the factions of New York, the spokesmen of those "organizations," each time, as they alternately took the initiative, pointedly assumed to represent *the* Democracy of the Empire State, and the assumption was, on the other hand as pointedly resented, while this internecine war was enjoyed as a good joke by the assemblage. Motions to adjourn followed half a dozen of the last ballots, and the Buchanan men, up to the thirteenth test, resisted any delay, with vehemence; but losing confidence in their ability to rush matters through, their ardor gradually cooled; and Pennsylvania, after the fourteenth ballot, seeing that they might soon be coerced into adjourning, caved in, with as good grace as possible, yet with a wry face; and it was the understanding at the time of adjournment, that the shrewdest of the Buchanan men were not so sure of sudden victory as they had been earlier in the action.

Fifth Day – June 6

Buchanan Nominated!

The President: The convention will now proceed to the fifteenth balloting for a candidate for president.[21]

When New Hampshire was called, Harry Hibbard rose to address the convention. There was a sudden calm, and his words were listened to with profound attention. He said:

Mr. President: The time has come when the New Hampshire delegation deems it a duty that she owes to her distinguished son and to the Democratic party, to yield her cherished preferences for that statesman, and to withdraw his name from the convention. I therefore withdraw the name of Franklin Pierce as a candidate for the presidency, [applause] and without making any ungraceful distinctions among the statesmen whose names are in nomination. New Hampshire desires to express her preference for her second choice—Stephen A. Douglas, of Illinois. [Immense applause]

FIFTEENTH BALLOT

	BUCHANAN	PIERCE	DOUGLAS
Maine	7	1	0
N. H.	0	0	5
Vermont	0	0	5
Mass.	10	0	3
R. I.	4	0	0
Conn.	6	0	0
N. Y.	17	0	18
N. J.	7	0	0
Pa.	27	0	0
Dela.	3	0	0
Md.	8	0	0
Va.	15	0	0
N. C.	0	0	10
S. C.	0	0	8
Ga.	3	0	7
Ala.	0	0	9
Miss.	0	0	7
La.	6	0	0
Ohio	13½	2½	6½
Ky.	4	0	7
Tenn.	12	0	0
Ind.	13	0	0
Ill.	0	0	11
Mo.	0	0	9
Ark.	0	0	4
Mich.	6	0	0
Fla.	0	0	3
Texas	0	0	4
Iowa	2	0	2
Wis.	5	0	0
Calif.	0	0	0
Total	168½	3½	118½

Ohio gave Cass ½ a vote, California 4.

SIXTEENTH BALLOT – Buchanan, 168; Douglas, 122, Cass, 6.
After the result had been announced—

Colonel William Preston, of Kentucky, evidently laboring under much mental agitation, said: I have been a devoted personal and political friend of the distinguished Senator from Illinois. But I appeal to the friends of Stephen A. Douglas as I have appealed to myself already, whether justice to that states-man and devotion to the Democratic Party does not demand that his name should now be withdrawn.

FIFTY VOICES: No! no! Sit down—ballots! ballots!!

I am sure that I represent the views of the best friends of Mr. Douglas, and I do not speak without knowledge, (looking toward William A. Richardson and then toward the speaker)— I do not say this without knowledge, sir. [Intense sensation]

Richardson of Illinois: Mr. President!

Innumerable Voices: Sit down! We want the ballot and noth-ing else!

Colonel Preston: I move that the gentleman from Illinois have consent to speak. The convention with but three dissenting voices gave its consent to the delegate from Illinois.

Richardson now rose amid the half-suppressed evidences of the wildest excitement, and said, Mr. President, I am far from advising—

Voices from Kentucky and Missouri delegations: Don't withdraw Dug—Stop!

Mr. Richardson, (waving down the excited crowd that gathered round him) Mr. President, I shall say what I would, and I am far from advising any man what he shall do at this hour.

Voices: Don't withdraw Douglas!

Richardson: But I feel I have imposed upon me a duty to—

A voice from Missouri seats: D—n the duty, sit down there.

Richardson: A duty to Stephen A. Douglas as well as to our common cause. [Cheers] As a friend to that statesman, I feel that I cannot advance his interests or the success of the party, by continuing him in this contest. [Cheers and loud demonstra-tions of dissatisfaction]

I beg to have read this telegraphic dispatch received last night from Washington—after its reading, *I shall withdraw Douglas from this contest.* [A confused scene of applause and dissatisfaction]

Telegraphic Dispatch from Douglas

I see in the telegraphic dispatches in the newspapers that there is danger of an embittered spirit in your convention. I wish you and all my friends to remember that the ascendency of our principles is a thousand fold more important than my own elevation. If the withdrawal of my name will ensure harmony, I beg you not to hesitate to take the step. My highest wish is granted if the convention is unanimous for the platform that embodies the principles of the Democracy of the Republic.

[Wild cheers for "Little Dug."]

If the nomination of Mr. Pierce or Mr. Buchanan, or any other of the Democratic statesmen named for the office can be secured by your aid, I beg that he may receive it. I earnestly hope you will give him first a vote of two-thirds, and then a unanimous vote. [Applause] Let no personal consideration disturb the unanimity of the convention.

S. A. Douglas

The reading of the letter was followed by a general rising of the delegates from their seats, and prolonged cheers.

On the seventeenth ballot the chair allowed great latitude to the speakers, who gave vent to their feelings as each state was called, and on the vote by states BUCHANAN WAS UNANIMOUSLY NOMINATED!

There were many wry faces, but party drill was irresistible, and for the candidate as for the platform, the vote of each state was "unanimously aye." The vote of Maine was cast with simple earnestness.

Harry Hibbard spoke for the last time for New Hampshire. He said she had faithfully adhered to Pierce, her first choice, until it was apparent that he was not the choice of the convention. Then she had withdrawn his name, and gone heartily for her second choice, the giant of the Northwest. And now, convinced that Buchanan was the choice of the majority of the convention, she went no less heartily for him. And he pledged for her a good fight for the nominee. She would send down her majority like an avalanche from her granite mountains. [Cheers]

Ben Butler for Massachusetts said that her Democracy, through their delegates, had shown by their steady vote the inflexibility of their convictions. They had given Buchanan votes, though not the entire number, all along, and now would go for him in a body. "Thirteen votes for James Buchanan." They would have a hard fight in Massachusetts, but whether they could succeed in storming the enemy's batteries, or not, they would, as a gallant son of that state said at Lundy's Lane, "We'll try sir!" . . .

Softs and Hards, of New York, rolled in together. William H. Ludlow, the Soft who had held on to Pierce as long as there was life in him, and had then gone for Douglas, proclaimed that there was to be no factious opposition to the nomination in New York, so far as the Softs were concerned. The Hards had been heartily for Buchanan all the time, and no new expression of faith was required of them. Those who had been bitterest against Buchanan, were now most anxious to swim with the current.

The chairman of the South Carolina delegation said: The delegates from South Carolina gave their votes first for Pierce and afterwards for Douglas, and so continued to do, as long as they were sustained by their immediate friends. But there is one thing of more importance than personal preference—the Constitution. To preserve the Constitution and the Union, we yield our choice of men and give our votes for James Buchanan.

The chairman of the Georgia delegation: The delegates of the State of Georgia come here pleased to do battle for Franklin Pierce. Next to him they preferred Stephen A. Douglas, as the defender of the Constitution. But it is not Pierce and Douglas alone that they love. They have a warm heart for James Buchanan, to whom they now give their unanimous vote.

Mr. Richardson of Illinois: I am instructed by the delegates to return to this convention their grateful acknowledgments for the complimentary vote which it has given to her distinguished and favorite son, by which he has received one hundred and twenty-two votes for the highest office in the gift of this great people. But it is not alone in this that honor has been paid to him. In all the great matters of principle which have been embodied in the platform of this convention, every member has endorsed the policy of Stephen A. Douglas. While the vote is complimentary, any man on earth might be proud of the measures of which he is the author, and the principles for which he has battled—and he is proud. But we believe the strength of the Democracy is in the principles more than in the man; and we say to our fellow Democrats, that as, in times past, the Democratic flag has never been torn in Illinois, so it will not be in November next. . . .

Colonel Samuel W. Inge, of California: California came here for a single purpose, and for the accomplishment of that purpose had instructed her delegates to go unitedly for one man, because she believed him to be favorable to a measure of great importance to her—the construction of an overland communication between the Atlantic and Pacific states. From the acts of the delegation from his own state, however, they have been given reason to suspect that they have been mistaken, sir; we look upon the acquisition of California to have been one of the greatest achievements of American arms. We—

The President: The gentleman is out of order. He will either continue his remarks to the subject of the vote of his state, or surrender the floor.

[Cries of leave, leave, let him go on.]

A motion was made and carried to permit the delegate from California to proceed in his remarks.

Mr. Inge: We have come far, braving the fiery sun and deadly malaria of the tropics to meet our brethren in this convention. We come from a great and rich country yet in its infancy, but for the acquisition of which much of American blood and treasure have been expended. From the days of Jefferson the desire to own it has been felt. California is acquired. She is before you by her representatives, pleading her vast commercial and agricultural resources. There she lies, surrounded by her sparkling sands hiding her golden treasures, worthy to be the admiration of the world. To her an overland communication with the Atlantic states is a matter of the first importance. As it is, she is severed from the Union by vast oceans, by a pestilential isthmus where civil war rages, by inhospitable and almost impassable deserts. Her delegates had been instructed to vote for James Buchanan, and would have done so, had it not been for the action of the State of Pennsylvania in voting against California's part of the platform. She would cast her vote for Buchanan now, because she did not believe that he was represented on the Pacific Railroad question by the Pennsylvanians in the convention. And he pledged the Pacific shores to re-echo the shout of triumph that would go up from the Atlantic states, and roll over the West, North, and South, for James Buchanan.

John L. Dawson, of Pennsylvania, took the floor. He would express his high appreciation of the honor now about to be conferred on Pennsylvania, and spoke in very flattering terms of Lewis Cass, with whose name the pages of history would be luminous; and of Douglas, the bold and powerful active statesman of the Democratic Party, who was young, but covered with honors; of Jesse Bright, of Indiana, whose high qualities made him the worthy representative of the mighty West; and Pennsylvania was especially flattered, that the towering greatness of her Buchanan had been recognized and had found favor in that convention.

ENDORSEMENT OF FRANKLIN PIERCE

Mr. Dawson had concluded his elegantly worded remarks, and taken his seat, without mentioning the name of Mr. Pierce at all, during his eulogies on the Democratic nominees for the presidency, when he was reminded of the omission, and rose again, and said that President Pierce had been true to the letter and spirit of the Constitution, and true to the cardinal principles of the Democratic Party, and the Democracy of the Union say to him this day, "Well done, good and faithful servant." [Loud applause.]

Benjamin F. Hallet of Massachusetts, Collector of Customs at Boston: At this stage I desire to introduce a resolution that will embody the sense of this convention on the administration of the present chief magistrate, for he believed that he but echoed the sentiment of the Democracy of the Union, when he said that the administration of Franklin Pierce will stand for ages as a model administration. [Loud cheers with slight dissent.]

Mr. George W. Peck, of Michigan, after a hard struggle got the floor, and said: Mr. President, I will not let the vote on this endorsement go to the country without my indignant protest. [Great confusion, and an effort to cry down Peck.] I shall be heard sooner or later. I beg to dissent from this vote—while I concur in the main with the resolution of honor to President Pierce. I will say that I do not honor him for his treatment of the great Northwest. I will not—as a delegate from the Northwest, whom he has abandoned to the perils of the navigation of the inland seas of the continent, [Applause and dissent] for the improvement of which he has forbidden the people, through their representatives, to appropriate the people's money. [Applause from the Western states.]

THANKS OF PENNSYLVANIA

Mr. Samuel W. Black, of Pennsylvania, rose and after the cheering for Buchanan had subsided said: Mr. President, Pennsylvania needs cheering no longer, I am appointed by the unanimous request of my state delegation to return thanks from the very heart of Pennsylvania for this unprecedented vote for her own beloved son. [Cheers] I will not make a set speech. But we do return you all our humble, but our earnest, sincere gratitude, for the honor this day received at your hands. . . .

Gentlemen, I said that I would not weary you with a set speech, and your kindling enthusiasm shall not make me forgetful; but one thing more and I will conclude.

I have become identified with the female movement on this floor [Laughter] from my support of the right of the ladies to the galleries. Now let me set Mr. Buchanan right on the matrimonial question. [Hurra! Hurra for old Buck] Though our beloved chieftain has not, in his own person exactly [Laughter] fulfilled in his own person [Renewed laughter] the duties that every man owes to the sex and to society, there is a reason. Ever since James Buchanan was a marrying man he has been wedded to the CONSTITUTION, *and in Pennsylvania we do not allow bigamy.* [The convention flings its hats to the ceiling.]

FLOURNOY'S APPEAL

Mr. T. B. Flournoy of Arkansas: Mr. President, I move that we now proceed to nominate a candidate for Vice-President. [Cries of no! No.] Sir, the most of us have impatiently watching for us from far distant homes, wives—lonely wives, Mr. President. [Cheers] Will you protract their sleepless vigils by a refusal to finish what little remains to be done, and let every delegate who has done his duty to society, and will not fail to do it again, fly on the steam cloud to the arms of the mothers of the Democracy of the Republic? [Intense cheering.]

On motion, the convention took a recess.

Afternoon Session

Pacific Railroad in the Platform

The chair called the convention to order promptly.

Mr. William Shields, of Missouri, offered the following resolution, which, under the rules, went to the committee on resolutions:

Resolved, That it is the duty of the federal government to construct, so far as it has Constitutional power so to do, a safe overland communication within our own territory between the Pacific and Atlantic states.

Mr. Horace T. Sanders, of Wisconsin, moved an amendment favoring the Pacific Railroad. . . . He spoke vehemently in favor of its adoption, in spite of calls to order by the chair, and by delegates, and a tempest of hisses and applause—managing to say very distinctly that the mighty Northwest would no longer permit her interests as a vast and prosperous and growing region of the country, to be stifled at the call of effete conservatism.

There were half a dozen motions and amendments confusedly piled one upon another so as to be unintelligible. At length a motion to lay the resolution with its amendments on the table was recognized. . . .

The motion to lay the above resolution on the table was defeated by the following vote by states—yeas, 74; nays, 220.

During this vote, South Carolina's vote was given, by mistake, in opposition to laying the resolution on the table, and the error was corrected with hot haste, showing that the little conservative state had frightened herself by the awful accident of being almost, by mistake, recorded as voting toward an improvement in the West. Alabama, after the states had all been called, having voted in the affirmative, came over and took her stand by the Northwest in opposition to the Southeast.

John S. Phelps, of Missouri, now in a highly excited manner, moved that the convention take a vote directly on the resolution. . . .

The vote on the adoption of the resolution was taken up, and resulted as follows . . . : yeas, 205; nays, 87.

The announcement of the result of this vote was wildly cheered. . . .

The study of the vote by states during this struggle is full of interest; it shows politicians in a state of perplexity quite amusing to outsiders. Pennsylvania, following the illustrious example of her son of towering distinction, trimmed, fearing to offend the ultra South by going for the road, or the far West by going against it, so her delegation dodged by dividing, the lion's share of them going with the South.

The Vice Presidency

Charles A. Wickliffe, of Kentucky, nominated Linn Boyd for the vice presidency. Thomas L. Harris, of Illinois, was instructed by the delegates from that state to present the name of a distinguished gentleman as the candidate for the vice presidency, . . . the man who was the first to plant the victorious American flag on the famous Hall of the Montezumas—need he name John A. Quitman! [Tremendous cheering.]

Louisiana nominated John C. Breckinridge, which movement was greeted with great applause. *Mr. Breckinridge:* With your leave, Sirs, Mr. President and gentlemen of the Convention. . . . I hold that unless there are very especial reasons for having it otherwise, promotion should follow seniority, and I beg leave therefore, most respectfully to decline to be a candidate. Why? I have been among those instrumental in bringing out the name of a distinguished gentleman from my own state. . . . Besides Sir, I am already a nominee—a candidate on the electoral ticket of Kentucky, and propose during the coming campaign to tread her valleys and climb her mountains in the laborious but delightful task of doing battle for your platform and your ticket. . . .

An Alabamian, whose speech could not be heard, nominated Benjamin Fitzpatrick of that state for the vice presidency.

Ex-Governor Aaron V. Brown of Tennessee was also nominated. Among other recommendations, it was stated he was a friend of Andrew Jackson.

James A. Seddon, of Virginia, was named as a candidate by a South Carolinian, and made a very thankful speech, in which he declined the honor. He thought it due the dignity of Virginia, from the position she had taken in this convention, not to have a son of hers upon the ticket.

W. W. Avery, of North Carolina, nominated James C. Dobbin. . . .

Georgia nominated Hersel V. Johnson, stating that not since the time of Jackson had she had a candidate for the presidency or vice presidency, or a single member of the cabinet. And she thought herself entitled to some consideration from this convention.

When the vote of states was called, Maine presented Thomas Jefferson Rusk, of Texas, with eight votes. A Texan felt himself authorized to withdraw the name of Rusk and did so.

Mr. Gove Saulsbury, of Delaware, nominated James A. Bayard, of his state, for the vice presidency.

Mr. Willard Saulsbury, of Delaware, nominated that distinguished Democrat of Missouri, Trusten Polk.

Mr. John S. Phelps, Missouri, highly appreciates this compliment to her distinguished citizen, coming as it does from his native state; but that gentleman had already been placed in nomination by the Democracy of Missouri for the governorship of the state. He was already in the field, and the Democracy of Missouri could not spare him for any other post. He begged, therefore, that his name might be withdrawn. . . .

FIRST BALLOT FOR VICE-PRESIDENT—Quitman, 59; Boyd, 33; Fitzpatrick, 11; Brown, 28; Dobbin, 13; Johnson, 32; Breckinridge, 55; Bayard, 31; Polk, 5; Butler, 27; and Rusk, 2.[22]

When Vermont was called, Mr. David A. Smalley said: The delegation of Vermont, believing that no Democrat has a right to refuse his services when his country calls, has instructed me to cast the five votes of Vermont for the talented, accomplished, and eloquent son of Kentucky, John C. Breckinridge.

The Second Ballot for Vice-President—The following was the result of the second ballot before the delegation made a stampede upon Breckinridge, Tennessee leading the way, and gave the young Kentuckian the unanimous vote . . .: Quitman, 24; Brown, 13; Dobbin, 11; Johnson, 22; Breckinridge, 117; and Butler, 51.

The scene that occurred between the first and second ballots was extraordinary. As the call of the states progressed, it was clear that Breckinridge was rapidly leading the other candidates, but the feeling for the young Kentuckian blazed suddenly into an universal enthusiasm, and half a dozen states were up at the same moment demanding to change their votes from Dobbin or Quitman, Johnson or Brown, to Breckinridge. All these changes were prefaced by sentences shouted above the din, hot with devotion to the withdrawn, burning with admiration of the adopted candidate. And so the tide of glory rose round the young man till he was nearly whelmed in the congratulations, and the continued cheering—caught up and echoed by the cannon outside—and by the embraces of half a thousand enthusiastic men.

When, after exhausting efforts, the president could be heard, he said: Gentlemen of the convention, John C. Breckinridge, of Kentucky, has received 296 votes and is therefore the unanimous choice of the convention for the office of Vice-President of the United States.

Then again the convention resolved itself into a carnival, a din as of an army entering a Malakoff,[23] hats and handkerchiefs waived in air—all dignities and proprieties waived altogether.

Finally a hoarse cry for Breckinridge! Breckinridge take the stand! ! organized itself from the multitudinous discord, and gathering volume, rose until the Kentucky delegation took the nominee by the shoulders and placed him where all could see and hear. The marvelous ovation hardly left him the self-control for speech, but Mr. Breckinridge said:

Speech of Breckinridge

Mr. President and gentlemen of the convention. This result is quite as unexpected to me, as it can be to any in all this space. In the inferior and personal aspect of this extraordinary manifestation, I beg you to consider all said that gracefully should be. I have no words to voice the gratitude that is welling from the innermost—[most enthusiastic cheers] from the innermost heart of me to the Democracy of the nation for this confidence.

There is one personal satisfaction that lightens this hour and fearfully accumulates responsibilities. [Subdued applause.] I derive that satisfaction from the reflection that, through all the balloting I have freely followed my political preferences nor professed a sentiment, nor softened an expression for a personal result. [Applause] He (Breckinridge) of an hour since, refused to ask for or accept the honor he knew he was unworthy of, but the Breckinridge created by the fiat of the Democracy to second its illustrious standard-bearer, had no choice but to serve. [Cheering everywhere.]

It is not proper for me to speak of the second man on your ballot; but of the chieftain I may. James Buchanan is one of the last of the survivors of the gigantic race of American statesmen whose deeds may not be separated from the glories of the Republic. Reserved to a green old age he has lived down detraction, and time has destroyed calumny. [Applause] Composed and dignified on this moral elevation, he is about to be clothed with the insignia of the chief magistracy of the nation! [Repeated applause.]

Gentlemen, I heartily concur in the platform you have affirmed. I endorse your resolutions. I am known to be a states' rights Democrat. [Applause]

Strong in the principles of Jefferson, enforced by the irresistible temper of Jackson, the people will entrust the men you have named for their government. I hope, in that event, I shall never forfeit the confidence of the Democracy of America. [Prolonged applause.][24]

*   *   *

The thanks of the convention were then returned to the secretaries of that body and to the citizens of Cincinnati. . . .

Loud calls were made for a speech from the chairman. He addressed the convention a short time, thanking them for the unexpected honor conferred upon him, congratulating them upon their choice of candidates, and upon the happy result of their arduous session. After his speech the hall was soon vacated —the Democracy dispersed.

POINTS IN THE CONVENTION PROCEEDINGS

Our report of the proceedings in the Democratic convention yesterday, is very full, and will, we think, be found fair and complete. There were, however, a few points worthy of special and immediate mention. When Buchanan was declared the nominee, and the thing to be done was for the delegates to rise to their feet and cheer—to assume that much enthusiasm, even if they had it now—the ultra South, preserved their dignity and their seats, and held their hats. The words of South Carolina in casting her votes after Pierce was withdrawn, were "Eight votes with *enthusiasm* for Stephen A. Douglas." The opposition of the South to the withdrawal of the name of Douglas was quite tempestuous, and it required the firmness of Richardson, backed by the letter from Douglas, to face the music. It was a sad showing for Pierce at first, that in order to be nominated by the North, his personal friend, Hibbard, from his own state, had to do it for him; and again, that no one could condescend to offer a resolution endorsing his policy in flatulent phrase, but one of his own fat office holders—Hallet, Collector of Customs at Boston. Then when this resolution was passed, the delegations from South and North Carolina, and one or two other Southern states, rose and made a melancholy attempt to get up a furor, giving a very feeble shout, and resuming their seats without sympathy in action or spirit. It may become evident after a time that it will not pay for Northern men to sell themselves to the South. The illustration presented in the case of Pierce, with his throat cut and his back broken, may be worth something.

THE PRESIDENCY — NOMINATIONS PAST AND TO COME

We stated, a few weeks since, that, in our opinion, the Honorable Salmon P. Chase and the Honorable Stephen A. Douglas were the most generally recognized representatives of the principles and policy of the parties to which they severally belonged, and that, as such, it was the duty of the leaders of those parties, in order to place the great issue of the day fairly before the ultimate tribunal—the people—to put them in nomination for the presidency[25]. . . .

We have been accustomed to look upon Mr. Douglas as the truest representative of the principles and policy of his party, and *therefore,* as its strongest man. . . . In the nomination of the

Honorable James Buchanan, the Democratic Party has opened its campaign with a retreat. . . . We were in favor of Mr. Douglas, because we love a fair stand-up fight—because his nomination would be a tender to the other party of the true issue to be tried before the great popular tribunal—because, bad as he is, we had rather see him President than Mr. Buchanan—having quite as much confidence in his integrity and more in his ability. The one might rise from the politician to the statesman; the other never was either. All his life a mere appendage to some party, the only effect of the brilliant opportunities which he has enjoyed, has been to demonstrate his total want of all elements of greatness. . . . The selection of Mr. Buchanan is in itself an equivocation—his only quality being the absence of all qualities. In the present state of political questions he is, to all intents and purposes, a new man—as much so as Mr. James K. Polk and General Franklin Pierce, or any other gentleman who might have been sprung upon the recent national convention, to harmonize the jangles of the Democracy. Who knows where he is? He is placed, it is true, upon what is called a "platform" —a collection of politico-literary absurdities and enormities, in the name of which damnable deeds have been committed, and may be again; but what idea to the people of this Union does the name of James Buchanan suggest? None.

RATIFYING THE NOMINATIONS AT WASHINGTON

The Washington *Union* publishes the proceedings of a meeting holden in that city on Saturday evening last to "ratify" the Cincinnati nominations, at which, with a refinement of cruelty worthy of a darker age, poor old Cass, stupid Pierce, and bitter Douglas were hauled forth to amuse the crowd by a hollow pretence of happiness at the auspicious result.[26] Cass, who had seen himself stripped of the last hope of that for which he had toiled and trimmed and equivocated a whole life long—Douglas, who with remorse gnawing at his heart, had just heard that his hated rival had put his foot upon his neck and sealed his disgrace by his discomfiture—Pierce, who had, at last, opened his eyes to the practical results of a course of infamy—drawn forth, like culprits by a tyrant party, to an exhibition more pitiful than that of the blinded Samson—not permitted even to bow their heads and in silence mourn over their desolation, but against their will made parts of a pageant—forced to be glad, and smile while all the furies were howling in their bosoms! Ah! How mankind revenges itself upon the demagogues. Their time may be delayed long, but it always comes; and terrible indeed is the retribution which it brings. Cass, Douglas and Pierce—what enemy could have inflicted so sore a punishment as that which they have received at the hands of their friends?

CHAPTER 4

Second Know Nothing Convention

‡ ‡ ‡

THE TOM FORD PARTY

Tom Ford has turned up again, having just made his second appearance on the Philadelphia stage, in his famous and only part of "Bolter," in the tragical-historical-tragical-comical-historical-pastoral-farcical drama of the *Dark Lantern*.[1] The solitary fact in his political history, antecedent to his nomination for lieutenant governor, was, that in June last, he bolted from the Know Nothing national convention. Having bolted once with success, what so natural as to repeat the operation? As one bolt had made him lieutenant governor, two might make him Vice-President. As two negatives are understood to be equivalent to an affirmative, two desertions from a party might constitute him the founder of a party. Tom Ford, the bolter, might, in the twinkling of a deck of cards, become Tom Ford the builder. And so our distinguished lieutenant governor, ceased for a season to pursue his study of parliamentary rules under the direction of the Ohio Senate, proceeded to the convention at Philadelphia, made bolt No. 2, and then became the architect of a party of his own. . . .

What is the object of—what good can come of a Tom Ford party . . . ? What that is desirable can be accomplished by a convention of the mutilated fag-ends of a dying organization, in New York on the 12th of June? Once upon a time, when the brains were knocked out of a thing, death would follow in a reasonable space. Now, we have something both brained and disembowled, yet it mouths at us, and insists that it is intensely alive. We have heard of persons running a few steps after their heads were chopped off, but this thing of the tail and hind legs merely, of an animal entering regularly into a race, has heretofore been unheard of.

But there is no mystery about this matter. Speculators in politics have the vital tenacity of mud-turtles and water dogs. The design of those who are attempting to infuse life into a carrion organization is clearly to claim a reward for at last abating the nuisance. The "true Americans" propose to enter the political market. They expect to give their stock a fictitious value by holding a pow-wow in New York, and then get up a joint stock arrangement with the Republicans at Philadelphia. The consummation for which they devoutly hope and devotedly labor, is that they may attain a position sufficiently dignified to be asked to capitulate—to sell out for a share in the honors and prospective profits of candidacy. They will have on hand a beautiful candidate for the vice presidency—one schooled in presiding over the deliberations of the Ohio Senate.

But, if the Republicans are so indiscreet, or charitable, as to absorb, on any *terms,* those who may compose the 12th of June convention at New York, they will have undertaken the digestion of a quick and fatal poison. The delegates . . . at the national markethouse council, must, previous to admission into the Republican army, throw aside their commissions as officers, and go to work in the ranks; and before being permitted to enlist, they should undergo a process of purification—should be washed in vinegar and rubbed with sulphur, that they may bring no bad odors or foul infection into camp. The "distinctive principles" of Republicanism and Know Nothingism are irreconcilable. There is not only no honest sympathy between them, but they are absolute antagonisms, Republicanism embodies a living and righteous sentiment—is broad, generous and frank,

and walks abroad in the noonday light. Know Nothingism is
the impersonation of an offensive prejudice—is narrow, selfish
and secretive, skulking in darkness with mask and lantern. No
more than an individual can serve God and mammon, can he
be a Republican and a Know Nothing. Know Nothingism has
no business in the coming presidential fight. It is an outside
thing—let it crawl into its hole. It is a pernicious excrescence, a
"mil-dewed ear," blasting all that is wholesome with which it
is associated; and if it becomes necessary, in order to effect its
eternal annihilation to devote the approaching contest to that
especial purpose, we say amen, though Stephen A. Douglas
should win the White House.

THE BOLTING KNOW NOTHING
CONVENTION IN OPERATION

What It Proposes to Do

*Horace Greeley, Thurlow Weed, George Law and James Gordon
Bennett, For Fremont*

New York, June 12

The K. N. Bolters met here today and completed their organization as a convention. Singular to say, all the Northern
states but Ohio are largely represented. Some of them have sent
up a crowd of delegates and representatives, to make an outside pressure.[2] New Jersey has a regiment of lobby members on
hand trying to get up a fever for Commodore Robert F. Stockton, who some time since, you recollect, made a bid for the
presidency, or rather another bid, as he has for a long term of
years been trying to be a candidate. It is not likely however,
that he will succeed now. The New England states are heavily
represented, in which fact, taken in connection with others
which I have not time to specify, may be discovered the finger
work of Senator Henry Wilson, Mr. Speaker Nathaniel
Banks & Co. . . .

The convention is determined to nominate somebody and to
build a platform, whereon to stand and run. The platform will

be composed of a large amount of Free Soil, and a little K. N. 'ism under the specious title of Americanism, as Tom Ford's speeches were some time since. . . . Large numbers of politicians are foolish enough to think that the nomination of a man here will give him strength at Philadelphia. But I think that the reverse should, and probably will be the case. If a man is nominated here, the fact should damn him, unless he happens to be a very good man.

It is curious and instructive to observe the materials of which this body of "sordid hucksters" who want to be bid upon by somebody, is composed. Among the outsiders are Horace Greeley and Thurlow Weed, who have been at work busily as beavers and sly as moles, today, trying to make an arrangement, to have the business of the convention referred to a committee to confer with a committee of the Philadelphia convention — to adjourn over until after the Philadelphia performance, or do any thing to *fuse*. They go for harmony, policy, conciliation, courtesy, for patching up matters, for fixing the thing all right, for union for the sake of victory. George Law[3] is mixing in, and is in favor of a nomination. He of course, repudiates the convention that repudiated him. There is a rumor that he will be the nominee, with the understanding that he will withdraw his name in case John C. Fremont is nominated at Philadelphia. Many of the New Englanders are in favor of nominating Banks here, and as he is a fast friend of Fremont, it is taken as assured if he gets the nomination, that he will decline after the nominations are made at Philadelphia, in favor of that nominee. In this form—the nomination here of a man who will back out in behalf of the Philadelphia nominee—it is probable that the big fight will be made to kill this thing. It is the best thing that could be done. . . .

*   *   *

New York, June 13

This morning, on taking a first look at the Know Nothing convention now in operation here, I saw that I had been unduly impressed with the probable importance of the thing by those who described it to me, and by the extensive reports in the newspapers.[4] This I am particular to mention, because I expect that my letter reflected the exaggerated notion to which I have made reference. The hall in which the convention meets is not a large one and was by no means full, though free to everybody, and opening direct on Broadway. The delegates were usually of the unfledged, spread-eagle kind, those who fancy that there are no Americans beside Know Nothings, and who are as devout in their worship of Pope *Sam*,[5] as any Catholic is in his knuckling down to Pius IX. Some of them are smart, but a large number deeply tinged with greenness. The speeches are nearly all Free Soil, and the points that are most cheered, are references to the Kansas war and Senator Charles Sumner outrage. The only importance now attached to this thing, has been imparted in the effort to manage it. . . . It needed no management but a kick—perhaps not even that.

Yesterday I thought a ticket would be nominated here. But a change has come over the spirit of the caucus. A mortifying event which I could not have anticipated, has changed the scene. In the convention this morning, immediately after the call to order, a communication was read *from the chairman of the Republican national executive committee, which was appointed at Pittsburgh* on the 22d of February. He calls the attention of the convention to the call for the Philadelphia convention, and expatiates as to its breadth, suggesting that it covers all the ground, etc. The reading of this document produced a sensation, and was received with cheers and hisses, the former predominating. . . . The communication seemed to be understood by all but the Robert F. Stockton men as the solution of the problem presented by the convention. Few of them would have presumed to hope that the proposition for a treaty, a fusion, would come from the Republican Party. But there it was, with the signature of the chairman of the executive committee of the Republicans. . . .

The fact is the Republican Party should not have stooped to pick up a piece of carrion. There were no votes worth counting, and no moral force worth talking about, to back the convention. It should have been permitted quietly to solace itself by making a nomination. The worst that could have happened would have been the injury they might have done some good man by the unauthorized use of his name.

There are four elements here at work. First, George Law who is a silly old fellow with a long purse, and who wishes to be a great man, is dabbling in the muddy waters, and has managed by dint of gold, to bring up a full New York delegation, and some delegates from other states too; and these are blundering about trying to believe that they represent something tangible. Second, there is Commodore Stockton, another old fogy, with more money than brains, who has sent up a crowd from New Jersey, whose knowledge extends as far as the Camden & Amboy Railroad, but no further, and who are doing their best to bring about a nomination, thinking that if they can nominate the old Commodore, the Philadelphians will have to take him up. This shows the quality of sense they have. Thirdly, there is the Nathaniel Banks and Henry Wilson influence manifested in the flesh of some dozens of New Englanders, whose object, I believe to be, the manufacture of capital for Mr. Speaker Banks to be invested in the vice presidency.[6] Fourthly, Horace Greeley and Thurlow Weed have knit the fragments together with their managing wires, and propose to melt the whole mass down and pour it into the cauldron of the Quaker City. . . .

I am now sure that the small potato convention here will not nominate. It will *fuse*. It was for sale without reserve, and there being no chance for more than one bidder, of course it will come down, and an "arrangement" will be effected. May his Satanic Majesty have a place specially hot and sulphurous wherein to roast such humbuggery.

* * *

New York, Friday Evening, June 13

The K. N. bolters referred the communication of Edwin D. Morgan, chairman of the Republican executive committee, to a select committee, and took a recess. This afternoon they have been sitting with closed doors, the alleged reason for which proceeding is that some Fillmore men got into the hall this morning and made a disturbance. There was no great row, however, and the fact is these K. N.'s are unaccustomed to daylight, and begin to wince and blink so soon as it poured upon them. These "several small fry" were almost, if not quite, frightened at the importance the press was giving them, and have returned to first principles, resumed the old style—crawled into their hole to contrive ways and means to die easy, and to get the highest market price for their skins. . . . The object is to let them down easy and this Morgan has done with an unnecessary amount of grease. Having gone into secret session, my impression is that they will make no more disturbance—give no signs but those of woe.

The delegations that were not full made great efforts to procure substitutes and ring them into the convention whether they were Know Nothings or not. I learn that several individuals were picked up in the streets, and dragged in and made to serve as delegates whether they would or no. Such earnest efforts were put forth to fill vacancies, that those who were unfortunately impressed into service were in danger of losing, if they did not absolutely lose, their cravats and coat tails.

There has been hardly a word said about *Samism* in the convention. However dull of comprehension the delegates are, they can see that there is now an overshadowing question to be met, and that K. N. 'ism is "defunct in the abstract," so they console themselves by talking flashy stuff about the eternal and perfect beauty of their peculiar doctrines, and the certainty of their ultimate triumph with all that sort of thing, and profess to be anxious to go into the battle, to put down the niggerocracy unembarrassed by flank movements. But they wish the foul skeleton of their party to be the frame work of the great free state party. They aspire to leaderships, and would have those who contend for free labor in the new states that are looming in the horizon, to skulk in holes to make the fight. This will not do. These fellows must go into the ranks. What little there is of the Ohio delegation, is doing very well. They are doctoring the patient quietly. But one remedy would have been better than their physic, viz: to have given the thing scope and verge, and rope to have hung itself. "All the drowsy syrups" in the world would not have put it to sleep so suddenly and to be wakened no more, as to have let it alone.

I saw George Law's bust by T. D. Jones, the sculptor, the engraving of George Law which is posted through the country, and George Law himself today, and took a steady and studious look at each. The sculptor and engraver have made the most of their subject. But I recognized the man from having seen his bust. Jones is an exceedingly able and accomplished artist, and I have but one criticism to make on his bust of Law. The bust looks as if the man might do for president, but the man doesn't look as though he would do. To be candid, neither does he look much like a builder of the "armaments that thunderstrike the walls of rock built cities, bidding nations quake." He is a ponderous, old fellow, with a rather delicate nose, standing out sharply from the masses of florid flesh that compose his face, and it occurred to me that he would sweat prodigiously on very slight provocation. The artists have attempted to give him a striking appearance by arranging his hair in picturesque style, giving it a shaggy, wild bristle, like the mane of a rampant lion. But seen on the man, this *har,* though formidable in quantity, is not stormy in appearance, and instead of being black as Central Africa at midnight, as the prints would lead us believe, it is dingily gray, and brushed back without any "make up" to give a distinguished expression. If George lived in our town, we would take him for a heavy pork merchant, who had both slaughtered and eaten, shipped and digested, huge hosts of ye hog. He had a large amount of manliness in him before the New York *Herald* seduced him into becoming a politician, and there may be enough of common sense yet remaining to him, to direct the use of his immense fortune to nobler purposes than in carrying on a vain squabble for office, and the petty glories of a one horse politician.

Speaking of the *Herald,* I saw that destined to be immortal phenomenon, James Gordon Bennett, today. He is a tall, thin-faced, cross-eyed, white-haired, elegantly dressed, decidedly

Scotch looking man, who walks slowly carrying a cane in his right hand, and appears to be any thing but observant, yet watches, (with a strange faculty for reading riddles in men, and looking clearly through the mists of distance and time) not only the matters immediately around him, but the course of events throughout the world. Newspaperdom owes him much for his unexampled energy and enterprise in procuring the latest news, and giving the initiative to the peculiar impetus in this country to the rapid transmission of news. Bennett's *Herald* certainly inaugurated the system of newspaper correspondence from all the important cities of the world, and the now prevailing custom of reporting public meetings in full and promptly. And now, what does Bennett do in order to "distance all contemporaries"? Why orders of R. Hoe & Co., *two ten* cylinder presses, which will be larger than any ever yet built, and will cost thirty thousand dollars each!

*   *   *

New York, June 14

The telegraph has probably told you of the action of the Bolting K. N. convention, as there seems to be a determination to consider their proceedings significant rather than ridiculous.[7] The features of the proceedings today were the conclusion to continue in session until after the Philadelphia convention has made its nominations, a speech by the great live hoax, George Law, and an *informal* ballot. . . .

The amount of all this is, that this convention ventures to indicate its choice, and modestly ventures to suggest that such choice should be influential at Philadelphia, and determines to go through with the farce of *nominating its choice for a nomination,* and waiting for its confirmation. The game is for this convention to make it understood that Banks is their choice for president, with the view of giving him strength when he turns up at Philadelphia a candidate for the vice presidential place on the ticket. The thing is to be fixed by giving the *second* place on the ticket made at Philadelphia, to the man named for the *first* place here. That you perceive would be a beautiful compromise. When the glory and prestige of the speakership victory was fresh in the eyes of the people, not a few went so far as to talk of Banks for the presidency, and that gentleman, lacking self-appreciation perhaps, declined to make any effort to be a candidate, but pointed his long fingers at Fremont saying: *"There is the man."* Now it appears that he has a disposition to preside over the Senate instead of the House; having first pointed out the reputed head of the ticket, he has certainly a claim on the tail. The nomination of Fremont by the Philadelphia convention is here estimated as a fact wanting only time to be fixed. I am fully convinced that he will be victorious early in the action. There is a flood flowing in his favor that promises to sweep on to fortune . . . for vice president, Charles Sumner. . . .

*   *   *

New York, Sunday, June 15

The melancholy history of one-horse conventions does not, I am sure, furnish a parallel to the bare-faced humbuggery, the naked knavishness, the manifest impotence yet high-flown assumptions of the fragmentary Know Nothing specimen here holding forth. In selecting the delegates holding seats in this convention, not two thousand persons have been directly concerned, and by these delegates not five thousand votes are represented. The New York state convention, at which the thirty-seven delegates holding seats in this "national" caucus were appointed, was attended by but twenty-five persons, as I am very credibly informed. And after this manner the work of making delegates has been performed elsewhere. In two or three states, a few schemers, thinking that by controlling this convention they might acquire influence at Philadelphia, have concocted and sent up full delegations, with a sprinkling of outsiders, to make opinion. This has been costly in a pecuniary sense, as the coercive power of cash has been the only efficient agency in mustering the forces. Delegations that were not full, have been filled with the most unheard of unscrupulousness. The Know

Nothing jugglers have searched the hotels and ransacked the restaurants, to find persons who could be induced to serve as delegates, and who were sufficiently American to be able to speak the English language without a palpable foreign accent. Persons whom I know never were Know Nothings, and never will be, have been offered and urged to accept positions as delegates. The demand for men to fill vacancies has far exceeded the supply, yet these men talk about their Americanism, their patriotism, the terrific responsibilities resting upon them, the grave issues that they have to consider, how the eyes of their countrymen are upon them, how America expects every man of them to do his duty, how they are to fix the present "crisis," the necessity there is for Union, the excellence of harmony among those opposed to slavery extension, the imperative call to cast aside party preferences, the occasion that exists for forgetting personal predilections, and so on exaggerating the exaggerations to which grave deliberative bodies which have foundation in fact, are prone, and miserably caricaturing everything like genuine dignity, power, and devotion to country. Knowing perfectly well that they represent nothing, they assume to speak for the great mass of the intelligent people of America. They chatter incessantly about forgetting party and personal ambitions, when they are (and I presume they have sense enough to know it) the very embodiment of the dirtiest and most ultra partisan sentiment ever engendered—the fag-end of a fanaticism that prevents the very union of the people of the North which they profess to pray for and to be working to bring about. They know, and say, that the Pope is not the enemy that the people of the United States now have to be on their guard against. The stuff about "popery" and "foreignism," they perceive cannot flourish in the atmosphere that now covers the land. Instead of making flannel shirts for Fejee Islanders, they observe that the people have orphans at home to clothe. The bloody old Pope is a small potato compared with the "distinguished gentleman from Africa." The idea of being frightened about the insidious wiles of "foreign influence" while American-born citizens are shedding each others blood in Kansas, is preposterous. We must look at home and settle with each other. Yet the chairman of the Republican executive committee, gave significance to this gathering, not of eagles, or buzzards (for these are big birds) but of *crows,* by proposing to treat with them, in short making them an offer, and now they are hanging and grinning, and squirming with the exquisite sensations of undeserved personal importance; and propose to hang fire until after the Philadelphian labor is accomplished. It is enough to make an honest man sick to look upon such a spectacle. Yesterday, the convention having balloted informally, which mode of operation exemplifies beautifully the puerile character of the concern, adjourned over until Monday, and then will take a recess until the thing to be done at Philadelphia, is done, when this Apollo Hall (the place where the K. N.'s meet) will serve as a vent hole for the inflammatory stuff concentrated in disappointed candidates. That it will answer well in this respect, I have no doubt. And the greater the amount of heated and foul air that escapes here, the more satisfactory will be the sign of health in that which may be accomplished at Philadelphia. . . .[8]

CHAPTER 5

Republican Convention

‡ ‡ ‡

A PLAN FOR A COALITION — WHAT WOULD BE THE EFFECT?

WE HAVE, on several occasions, . . . stated that there is a probability that such nominations may be made by the fragmentary Know Nothing convention . . . as will be agreeable to the members of the Republican convention to be holden at Philadelphia, on the 17th, and that in such case they will be adopted and endorsed by the latter, and thus a coalition be effected which will largely increase the chances of the candidates of an election.[1] There have been as we are told, the emissaries of gentlemen willing to serve their fellow-citizens as incumbents of the presidential office, circulating through the West, with a view to promote such an arrangement, depicting, with no little vehemence and elaboration, the benefits of which it might be the source, and representing, with what approximation to the truth it is difficult always to determine, that this or that leading politician—including large numbers of that order of our fellow-citizens—is in favor of the plan and resolutely interested in its promotion.

[78]

In our opinion, the fact that a gentleman has consented to become the nominee at New York, should be one of the most conclusive of all reasons why he should *not* be nominated at Philadelphia. The Republican convention had better not meet at all than meet as an appendage to any other party body whatever—least of all to a Know Nothing council. The only legitimate strength of a political party is in the vitality of the sentiment upon which it is founded, and if in this respect, the Republican Party is reduced to a condition so destitute that it needs to commence its national existence as a parasite, it had better disband at once, and permit the materials of which it is composed to find their proper places under the influence of more potent laws of affinity. A nomination made in this wise might possibly bring out a very respectable candidate, but it would not be a Republican nomination, and would not so be looked upon. The process would be a virtual postponement of the Republican principle, and would alienate both in numbers and zeal upon the Republican side, far more than, by any possibility, it could gain upon any other; and in all probability its effect would be to ensure a well deserved defeat to the coalition by which the experiment was undertaken. . . .

*   *   *

The nominations of the Republican Party are yet to be made, and it remains to be seen whether its representatives are ready to imitate the example of their fellow citizens of the Democratic Party, and commence the campaign with a retreat.[2] Our opinion has been that they will do so; for of all creatures the most imitative is the politician, and we do not remember the commission of an act of folly by one party that the other was not instantly ready to follow so illustrious a precedent. We look upon the Republican sentiment as at this moment sufficiently potent to ensure a victory, if it is properly represented in a Republican man; but there are, we doubt not, very many excellent, old, cautious *party* politicians who think the contrary, and who dream of nothing but tactics and diplomacy, coalitions and compromises. From their point of view, a party success is

the one thing needful, for which sacrifices even of principle may
be made. . . . .

Where two parties are in the field, each having tampered
with its principles, the success of the one is just as desirable as
the success of the other. Between two organizations merely
struggling for possession of the government, he is either interested or foolish who has a choice. . . .

*   *   *

The trucklers, temporizers and compromisers, however, are
at work upon both sides.[3] Upon one the friends of Buchanan,
and upon the other, the discoverers of Fremont, are endeavoring, by their clamor, their puffery, and their plots, to avoid and
obscure the true issue—to set aside the real men, and to make
the contest as insignificant and negative in its vicissitudes, as its
result would be when it is reached. We do not believe, if the
question is reduced to this, that the people much care whether
Buchanan or Fremont, or Nobody, is elected to the presidency.
To us, and we doubt not to a great majority of them, the election of one of those characters—or of a fourth whom we had
liked to have forgotten—Fillmore—would be just as significant
as that of the other. Upon the important question of the day,
Messrs. Buchanan and Fremont stand upon equal grounds—
they are negatives. Their nomination would emasculate the
presidential campaign, and render the great and solemn trial
of the highest question in our politics a farce as ridiculous as
the drama of the Prince of Denmark, with the part of Hamlet
omitted.

COLONEL JOHN C. FREMONT

It is well known that for several months past an effort has
been made to bring this gentleman forward as a candidate for
the presidency.[4] At first the plan was to create a popular feeling in his behalf, and place him in nomination as an independ-

ent candidate, without a convention nomination, but there was no response to suggestions of this sort. Then the idea was started of making him the Republican candidate, and an extensive correspondence has been carried on from Washington with a view to that object. Mr. Thomas Hart Benton's late letter, stigmatizing the consistent efforts of the opponents of slavery and its extension and domination, as so degrading to the Senate as to make it an unfit place for men like himself, and proposing "a new man unconnected with the agitation," was part of this correspondence. Still further to prepare the way, we have now a letter from Colonel Fremont himself. Dates are curious things, and some attention to dates will throw a good deal of light on this letter. It seems that Governor Charles Robinson, of Kansas, wrote him in February. This letter is not published, but it was probably written about the same time that Governor Robinson and his associates sent to Governor Salmon P. Chase, Governor Myron H. Clark, of New York, and others, their appeal for sympathy and aid, to which Governor Chase, and upon his recommendation, the legislature and the people of Ohio so freely and generously responded. Colonel Fremont receives it at Washington, the center of the effort in his behalf. He made no reply at the time but several weeks afterwards in New York, composed the letter now published. What the reason for the delay was does not clearly appear. But the letter is a good letter, though it proposes nothing. It declares the writer's sympathy with the free state men of Kansas. It suggests, moreover, that in "contests and struggles," "if a man has good points, then they become salient and we know each other suddenly." The New York *Times* sees, in these words, a description of Colonel Fremont himself. "His good points," says the *Times,* "have become salient in it, (the letter,) and we know him suddenly." Perhaps the letter was intended to reveal "the new man." We are glad that it is printed. We are glad that the devotion of Colonel Fremont to "Freedom and the emancipation of the country from the rule of an unscrupulous and oppressive oligarchy," which the *Times* informs us was heretofore only known to "his intimate friends," is at length declared. Colonel Fremont's character and qualities are such as make his accession of value to any cause. His successful speculation in California has also made him enormously rich, and he can afford to spend money freely for any object which he deems worthy of attainment. But the idea of making him a candidate for the presidency for reasons like these, is simply absurd. It will be time enough to think of that when he has served in the ranks awhile, and given proof by continuous acts of earnest, open and persistent devotion to the cause of Liberty. A TRIED MAN, and NOT "a new man," IS WHAT THE COUNTRY WANTS.

*   *   *

Undoubtedly I may be much deceived, but I will confess to total inability to read the signs of the times this time, if the Fremont movement fails to carry everything before it at Philadephia.[5] Fremont is not the first choice of a majority of the convention, but *is the second choice of nearly everybody.* William H. Seward and Salmon P. Chase each have many ardent friends; and I think it is generally conceded that the latter more truly than any other man represents the free state side of the controversy as the fight should be made. But no man in the Union has been so misconstrued, so misrepresented, so misunderstood as Chase. While he is the ablest and truest Jeffersonian Democrat alive, and a gentleman spotless in private life, nearly half the people imagine that he is a pirate. And there are many who hold that the power of the prejudices against him, facts dying out it is true, yet still having some force, would in the precarious battle coming on, turn the scale against the forces of freemen, were he the bearer of their standard. It may be that a change will come over the spirit of affairs at Philadelphia, but from this standpoint I can gather no presidential portents but the mutterings of a Fremont tempest. Mr. Chase will, however, be stronger in the convention than I considered probable, when writing a few days since. He will have some New England votes, and it is anticipated that many will turn up for him from the Northwest, though there is a singular want of knowledge of the preferences of delegates belonging in that quarter. Some of the Ohio delegation, who were presumed by those who sent them, to be Chase men, have the Fremont fever so badly that it is questionable whether they will not go for him on the first ballot. The second choice of the New Yorkers, the first being Seward, of course, is Fremont. And just so it is with the Chase men generally. After Chase and Seward, the fight is between Fremont and Judge John McLean, of Ohio, the Young Americanism and the Old Fogyism, of the free state party, and in a convention, most of the delegates to which are young men and new men in politics, you will not be long in calculating who will win. And then, with Young America—in a sense not unwholesome either—in the field against Old Fogy Know Nothingism, with the scales on its eyes, and the tail feathers of the American eagle in its teeth, with a fat man accidentally famous and now fresh from the Pope for leader, and also against that queer amalgamation between federalism and filibusterism, the Douglas Democratic Party, with "not simply James Buchanan" but its "representative" to lead it in such a triumphant war, who would win? But if Fremont is nominated, Charles Sumner must go with him. Nathaniel Banks will not do. He was more than half-spoiled by his election to the speakership, and his availability, as well as his excellency, is questionable. The objection to Sumner for the vice presidency comes from New England and chiefly from Massachusetts. It is asserted in that quarter that they want Sumner to continue to be an active Senator—they do not wish him buried in the vice president's chair. Before the assault upon him by Preston Brooks, it was doubtful whether he could be re-elected, and the general impression was that he could not; now, however, his re-election by almost a unanimous vote is absolutely certain. The overwhelming propriety of making Sumner the presiding officer of the Senate, is however, recognized, and that it will be irresistible at Philadelphia I am confident. It is even urged as a strong objection to the nomination for the presidency of Chase or Seward, that in such an event it would not do to run Sumner for the vice presidency, as two freesoil senators upon one ticket would be starting out "too steep." The New England objection is overthrown by the fact that, as a practical man, Mr. Sumner has not been of much consequence in the Senate. He was a gigantic exquisite in person, and as an orator, his harangues were like the extravagant edifices erected by the merchant princes of this city—too fine for good service. But he would make a most thoroughly informed, impartial and accomplished presiding officer.

John C. Fremont resides in this city in very handsome style, and is a middle-sized gentleman, with a fine, frank face, bright with intellectuality, and full of pluck. His complexion has been so sun-burnt and frost-blistered in his adventurous journeyings, that though he has lived some time in the shade, it looks as if excessively bronzed by recent exposure. The objectionable point in his personal appearance is that he *parts his hair in the middle*. That is certainly awful, but I can't help it.

First Day – June 17

McLean and Fremont

This is the morning of the first day of the Philadelphia convention. . . .[6]

The New York convention has done up its work beautifully. I could not have recommended a more satisfactory performance. All of its "informal" candidates, will, I am told, decline the honor of a nomination from such a source.

As for the Philadelphia convention—the hotels are full, caucuses have been held nearly every hour in the last twenty-four hours. The quiet of this intensely respectable Philadelphia people is disturbed. Scores of the Republican members of Congress are here. General Henry Wilson, Joshua R. Giddings, and Nathaniel P. Banks, are among the number—Horace Greeley and Thurlow Weed are also here.

The Fremont feeling is strong, but is not so overpowering as I had anticipated. Mr. Salmon P. Chase has numerous warm and active friends, but many from the Northeast, think that if a first class free soil statesman is brought out it should be William H. Seward. When Greeley and his disciples talk about the want of availability of the free soil statesmen, they mean that Seward is not available, and are right, and they wish to preserve him intact. In the Lawrence Hotel last night, the headquarters of the Ohio delegation, the Chase feeling was warm. The Ohio delegates stand one-half for Chase, and the other half divided between John McLean and Fremont. The Rhode Islanders are decided Chase men, and I might mention several parts of delegations that are in favor of Chase. But I do not think that Mr. C. can be nominated by this crowd. The struggle will be between the McLean and Fremont men; and the friends of Chase will as a general thing go for Fremont. The *conservative ticket* is: For President, McLean, for Vice-President, Fremont. The Fremonters are urged to be conservative and conciliating and go for McLean for President, and then the McLean men will go for Fremont for Vice President. The Pennsylvanians, slow, easy, respectable folks, are for McLean. The Philadelphia *Times* of this morning, has a leader on the responsibility and duty of the Republican convention. We quote:

"First and foremost, as an indispensable pre-requisite to success, is the nomination of a FIRST CLASS statesman for the presidency; one who is recognized as such by the whole nation, who would bring to that great office the fruits of a long experience in public affairs, and the pledge of a life of unsullied integrity and honor. For only such a man can there be any rational chances of success. . . . Public opinion points to one name as the man for the crisis; no living statesman stands so high in the popular affections and estimation as he; all the rare and elevated characteristics that the presidency demands he possesses; all the virtues that dignify and adorn the human character, he has exhibited in his long and honorable career."

You perceive we are approaching a climax. The next sentence is: "That man is John McLean, of Ohio!" And there spoke Pennsylvania. This is a great expanse of little red brick houses, with white window shutters, and they think it is the capitol of the United States; but it isn't. The constant assertion in behalf of McLean is: "He is the only man with whom we can carry Pennsylvania." This is met by the remark that he is the only man who would not carry Ohio. The people of the Western Reserve would not go for him, and the majority that elected Chase governor would be found missing. One of the prominent editors on the reserve says that the mass of the Free-Soilers there would throw their votes away on the regular old

Abolitionist ticket, rather than go for McLean. The Jersey folks say that Commordore Robert F. Stockton only can carry their state, and there are certain other states that can only be carried by particular candidates. This will do to talk, but not to base action upon. If there are several states, each of which can only be carried by a particular man, and a different particular man is indispensable to each state, why the convention should let itself down easy, and permit the nomination to slide....

Who Will Be Nominated?

We have every reason to believe that the nomination will be effected with less difficulty than was at first anticipated. The impression among the different delegates is that Judge John McLean, of Ohio, will be nominated for the presidency, and Colonel John C. Fremont, of South Carolina, for the vice presidency. Indeed, the warmest of the supporters of the different candidates for the nomination concede the ultimate success of the ticket above named, which is certainly one of the strongest character.

The New York delegation is 95 for Fremont to 10 for McLean. The number of delegates, you understand, is three for each congressional district. The Northwestern delegations are strong for Fremont. Caleb B. Smith made himself useful by making a long speech to the Indiana delegation, in favor of McLean. There is too much twenty-five year old Whiggery in that to suit my taste. The Philadelphia *Pennsylvanian* of this morning has the following squib:

"It is proposed, if Colonel Fremont's friends succeed in procuring him the nomination for the presidency, to head their ticket thus:

FOR PRESIDENT,
col. j. fremont, son-in-law of
THOMAS H. BENTON.

They hope to elect him by availing themselves of "Old Bullion's popularity."

Now this is a palpable imitation of the ANDREW JACKSON donelson joke, and then the fun of it is that Benton is supporting

Buchanan, the "favorite son," etc., and has quarrelled with his son-in-law. He don't speak to him, sir, not at all, sir! The story that Fremont had agreed to be the candidate of bolting Know Nothings, whether nominated at this convention or not, is this morning authoritatively contradicted. It was from the first a manifest lie.

The Girard and Lawrence Hotels are swarming after the manner of the Burnet at the Cincinnati convention. The crowd here is nearly as large, but not so noisy as that which gathered at the travail of Democracy in Cincinnati. There is but a slight quantity of liquor consumed, very little profane swearing is heard, and everything is managed with excessive and intense propriety. The most cautious conservative and devoted Union-saver, would be satisfied with the character of the men here assembled. The mass of them are not radicals and hotspurs, anxious to change instantly the face of the whole globe. The difficulty is that there is likely to be too much conservatism and consequent timeserving. As for confidence in success, the delegates do not speak as if the country belonged to them, as the representatives of Pierce-Democracy at Cincinnati were in the habit of doing—do not claim the Goddess of Liberty as a nigger of theirs—but they speak very freely of who will do for members of the cabinet, and for foreign ministers, as if the thing was fixed, and it were as easy to elect as nominate. . . .

Details of Proceedings

The convention . . . was composed of as excellent a class of men as ever assembled with high purposes of public policy. The Musical Fund Hall (twice as large, I think, as Greenwood Hall, Cincinnati,) was densely filled; the interest felt in the proceedings was intense, and the enthusiasm abounding and only too demonstrative. Notwithstanding the vast dimensions of the hall, the entrance to it was crowded to suffocation and in the street was a shifting multitude.

The convention was called to order by Edwin D. Morgan, of New York, who nominated the Honorable Robert Emmet for temporary chairman, who on being conducted to the chair, made the most clear and sensible, and the strongest speech I ever heard on such an occasion. . . .

Henry S. Lane, of Indiana, was chosen the permanent chairman of the convention. He was conducted to the chair, and stood forth on the platform—a man about six feet high, marvelously lean, his front teeth out, his complexion between a sun blister and the yellow fever, and his small eyes glistening like those of a wild cat. He "went in," and made the most astonishing speech ever heard in these parts. The New Yorkers, near whose delegation I sat, were first amazed, and then delighted, and throughout excessively amused and warmed up. They said —as he would fling his arms in wild gesticulation, and utter the most impassioned and swelling sentences, smacking his fists horribly at the close of every emphatic period, "bringing down the house" every lick in a tremendous outburst of screams, huzzas, and stamping—"*Western* all over." But he stirred the multitude as with a thousand sharp sticks, and if he doesn't have a national reputation soon, it will not be because he does not deserve having fairly won that much celebrity. Taken all in all, the speech made a good impression. Then the orator continued his "Westernisms," as the Eastern men called them, filled his mouth with tobacco, placed one leg over the table behind which he was seated, and put the votes and made his decisions in the most off-hand style imaginable, without rising, and infusing into everything a spirit of a peculiar humor that was irresistible.

It being announced that the committee on platform could not report that afternoon, and no ballot being in order until the platform was adopted, the rest of the time was occupied in making speeches, Caleb B. Smith of Ohio, Owen Lovejoy, of Illinois, and Senator Henry Wilson being the speakers. Wilson said that the representatives of the North at Washington, would do their duty, regardless of consequences; and was applauded to the echo.

The Fremont Fever

It was ascertained last night beyond a doubt that John Fremont had a clear majority of all the votes in the convention, and that his friends could nominate him if they desired to do so on the first ballot, but it was understood that they would not from motives of policy put him through on the first ballot. The friends, personal and political, of Mr. Salmon P. Chase, have under contemplation the withdrawal of his name, or rather the propriety of not permitting it to be used before the convention. Numbers of delegates elected as Chase men have been captivated by the star of Fremont. The counsels of Horace Greeley and Thurlow Weed have turned them over. These New York politicians, wish to keep Mr. William H. Seward nicely pickled away to turn up at some time auspicious to him, and they are afraid to do justice to *the* Republican statesman of the West, whom they know really to be a taller man than their idol, and a purer. New York politics is here, as everywhere, in the market. The young men have been enlisted in the Fremont cause, and the old fogies have gravitated to John McLean. The politicians of the East are for Fremont, because they think he will win. The prestige of coming victory is with him, and the camp followers are at his heels, of course. Pennsylvania wants the conservatism of Buchanan outdone, and McLean to do it, and New Jersey backs her, and one-third of the delegation of Ohio endorses her. Out of the sixty-nine delegates of Ohio, McLean has twenty-four. No one in Ohio suspected that would be the case. The Chase men being thus placed in a minority, will not, I think, permit his name to be used.

Attempt to Reorganize the Whig Party

The fact is that the McLean movement is an attempt made by the antediluvian Whigs who have been placed in Congress by the Republican movement, to reorganize the defunct Whig Party under a thin disguise of Republicanism, to consist solely of talk about the Missouri Compromise. But this will not do. The movement has spent its entire force in destroying Mr. Chase's chances in this convention. Now it will be killed outright and forever. The old Whigs, with moss on their backs, of Pennsylvania and New Jersey—those who were pretty fairly up in the ranks twenty-five years ago, and have been lagging ever since—say incessantly that they must have McLean, because he is a man of a more dead conservatism than Buchanan, to carry those states, and they want Fremont for Vice-President —that is, they are willing to give Fremont the vice presidency, if his men will go with them for the head of the ticket. And among the leaders in this movement, are a dozen prominent old Whig politicians of Ohio—Honorable John A. Bingham, and I believe, but am not yet certain, Honorable Samuel Galloway. The Allen Trimble men are for McLean. Their voice is heard, sobbing from the wilderness by the wayside, for sympathy. Assurances, pretending to be from authoritative sources, are given, that if McLean is nominated, Fillmore will withdraw, and South America go for McLean, a consummation to be devoutly dreaded and persistently shunned. An extensive and lively correspondence has been going on for some time between the old Whig politicians of the North and South, the pith of which was to devise a plan by which this convention could be made the means of resuscitating the Whig Party. Chief among these correspondents have been John Bell, of Tennessee, and Tom Corwin, of Ohio, Corwin urging Bell to allow his name to come before this convention as a candidate for Vice-President—McLean to be President. This scheme is broken down, however, because a majority of the delegates in this convention is composed of men with Democratic antecedents. The game, therefore, is to run McLean and Fremont through on the fast line. The McLean men were hot last night—in fact, almost desperate, and threatened combustion and explosion if their demands were not complied with. The talk was that a resolution nominating McLean and Fremont by acclamation would be offered. Bingham, of Ohio, did say that such a thing would be done, and that those who would presume to take the responsibility of opposing or defeating it, would do so at their political peril. The Washington atmosphere has had a bad effect on Bingham. The McLean and Fremont ticket by acclamation notion is of city of Washington origin.

McLean's friends are certainly very injudiciously and improperly and pertinaciously rampant, dogmatic, and exacting. I cannot think that the venerable Judge understands exactly the handle they are making of his name. They are quite too fast for fogies; that is, they *stick too fast*. The friends of Mr. Chase undoubtedly have the power to make Sumner the candidate for Vice-President, but I fear that they will not use it to that advantage, and that the illustrious sore head will be passed by for Cassius M. Clay, of Kentucky. This would be awfully bad policy, as well as the omission to perform an act of justice that would by virtue of the people redeem the Senate from everlasting disgrace, and in itself be a fact that would shine like a star forever in our history. There is, however, another idea afloat. There is a Mr. Dugan, or Dayton—Dayton I believe it is—who lives somewhere up country, perhaps in Jersey, whose antecedent is that he voted against the Fugitive Slave Law, whom it is said should be taken up to conciliate the McLean men if Fremont is nominated. Conciliations are the order of the day. The politicians are overriding the people. There is, as has been forced upon my observation, a striking similarity of feeling in favor of Fremont here, and that for Buchanan in Cincinnati. There was first the same kind of impression that Fremont was the man, and then the drift wood told the course of the current.

Second Day—June 18

FREMONT SUPPORT

The crowd in the convention this morning is excessive, and the hall, as the day is sultry with a slow rain, is oppressively hot. And I assure you the feeling is warm as the atmosphere. There are various threats to bolt in case certain things come to pass, from which fact you may judge of the state of the nerves. There are a few of the friends of Mr. Chase who go for McLean as their second choice, and but few. A large majority will go for Fremont. I have heard it suggested, though of course as a mere conjecture, that if Fremont were elected, Mr. Chase would be Secretary of State. Assurances have been received that if McLean is nominated Chase will stump the state of Ohio for him, speaking in every county. But even in that case, from all the indications that I have observed among the Western

Reserve men, and others, Buchanan would carry the state. In a party of gentlemen last night, a gentleman suggested that Fremont would be easily influenced by the Free Soil senators—that is, particularly under the care of William H. Seward. But a gentleman of our city, whose opinion is worth something on such a point, said that he had visited Fremont with the purpose of forming an opinion of the man, and had talked with him and talked with his friends, and his opinion was that if Fremont were elected, he would himself be *de facto* the President of the United States. He seemed to be a very quiet, very modest, exceedingly resolute man—he was not a big man, but had an intellectual and strong, manly face, and a complexion that would indicate that he had just come in from a thousand miles ride through the sun. His face was indelibly marked with exposure. It was said of Fremont that the only person in the world who had much influence over him was his wife, and that she is a most estimable lady, handsome, and intellectual, fond of her home, her husband and children, and devoted to them, and a strong anti-slavery woman, which, it is said, she learned from her mother, Mrs. Colonel Benton, who always differed from her husband on that subject.

The great and striking argument in favor of Fremont for the presidency, is, that he knows more about, and is more interested in the territories of the Union, than any other man, and that it would be the work and the glory of his administration to attend to their best interests, that they might become free and great. There is plausibility in this it must be confessed.

One of the notables of the convention is Francis P. Blair, of Maryland, the old friend of Andrew Jackson, and Hickory's thunderer through the press. He is a little old gentleman, thin, slender and feeble in appearance, yet moving about with considerable activity. The expression of his face is spoiled by a badly fitting set of false front teeth, which his upper lip is not able to hide. Then he is given a top-heavy appearance by the fact that his head is too big for his body, and his hat too big for his head. He is treated with distinguished consideration, and the mention of his name is invariably followed by uproarious applause. Indeed there is quite too much of this hammering and stamping and yelling in the convention.

Exciting Scenes—Withdrawal of McLean and Chase

The game of the McLean men today, was to force a union between the McLean and Fremont men.[7] That was their talk on every corner. As a specimen of the literature used to bring this about, I annex the following circular, which was handed every delegate on leaving the hall:

DELEGATES: You are assembled here to promote a great and holy cause. In this work there should be harmony, forbearance, freedom from mere personal or local influences. So only will there be success.

You are divided between McLean and Fremont. *Why not unite their names on one ticket?* It would be invincible. All the friends of both might go home satisfied. In the name of Liberty, of our country, and of God, do this, and you will deserve the applause and the blessings, as your nomination will command the support of

THE WHOLE NORTH.

The Honorable David Wilmot, from the committee on the platform, reported the resolutions. . . .[8]

Judge Rufus P. Spalding, of Ohio, rose and said he was about to withdraw the name of a good and great man and a pure patriot. [Great confusion.] The speaker then proceeded to read the date of a letter—"Cincinnati, June 14."

Cries, "Name," "name," "name!"

Judge Spalding then went on to read the letter, which was as follows:

I have repeatedly declared, as some of you know, that I have no desire for the presidency, and that I prefer my present position on the bench. From the partial estimate of my services and long experience in public affairs, my friends have supposed that I might be able to contribute, somewhat, to the adjustment of the exciting questions which now agitate the public mind, and threaten a dissolution of the Union. This consideration was presented to me, as a reason why I should not refuse to permit my name to be used with the names of others for the office of chief magistrate; at least so far as to ascertain some indication of the public opinion; and I consented, with the understanding that I might withdraw it at any time, without any imputation of unkindness to my friends. . . .

The time has arrived when a nomination is to be made for President. I perceive several names are to be brought before the Convention for that high office; and I desire to say to my friends that to accomplish the object above expressed will require a hearty and vigorous co-operation of all the elements of the party about to make the nominations; and if these shall be likely to combine more strongly in favor of any other person, I wish my friends to withdraw my name, without a struggle in the Convention. In such an event, I shall have done all that can be required of a citizen, and I shall feel no reproach. . . .

JOHN McLEAN

The announcement of Judge McLean's withdrawal caused a fierce sensation in the Pennsylvania and New Jersey delegations.

T. G. Mitchell made a very handsome speech, withdrawing the name of Salmon P. Chase, of Ohio, and reading the following letter from Mr. Chase:

My Dear Sir . . .

I need not say that I should regard a nomination for a distinguished position, by such a convention as that which will assemble on the 17th, as an honor not to be easily overvalued. But no one, perhaps, knows better than yourself how persistently and earnestly the labors of my political life have ever been directed to the promotion of the cause of freedom, progress, and reform, of which I trust the convention will prove itself a faithful guardian. The success of that cause is infinitely dearer to me than any personal advancement; and I should look upon any nomination for any office, however exalted, if prejudicial to it, as a calamity to be dreaded and avoided, rather than as a distinction to be sought and desired. At the present crisis, especially, when the policy of slavery propagandism, adopted by the existing Administration, has been formally sanctioned by the platform of the convention recently assembled at Cincinnati, when the free state of Kansas demanding admission into the Union is repelled by a party majority acting under the dictation of the slave power; and when the cries of free state brethren in Kansas, insulted, oppressed, despoiled, imprisoned and in imminent jeopardy of life, as well as liberty, are appealing to us for help, it would ill become any true friend of liberty and justice to allow any personal considerations whatever to stand in the way of that complete union which is essential to the redress of these wrongs. . . .

After the reading of the letter from Mr. Chase, and his personal withdrawal, there being no candidate before the convention but Fremont, it was proposed to nominate him by acclamation. But the McLean men having been taken by surprise by the reading of that gentleman's letter and his sudden withdrawal, were profoundly excited and wished time for consultation. They therefore insisted upon an adjournment. This, after a time, was granted; Moses H. Grinnell, of New York, mount-

ing the platform and favoring an adjournment, which was carried to five o'clock. In the interval, about four hours, was the
grand struggle of the convention. Several of the delegations
were in caucus. Pennsylvania, Ohio, and New Jersey were particularly excited. The Ohio delegation was in full blast, and the
McLean and Fremont men "talked right out in meeting". . . .

At last the caucus determined—though several of Mr. Mc-
Lean's most sincere and warm friends opposed it—to place his
name again before the convention, and make a fight upon it.
Those of his friends opposed to this said, "We cannot possibly
nominate him, and why should we set him up merely to be
knocked down, expose him but to have him slaughtered?" But
he was placed before the convention again, and an informal
ballot was had. This resulted in a vote of 359 for Fremont to
196 for McLean. The friends of the latter now solaced themselves with the reflection, which they assumed, that the withdrawal of McLean had been the act that had given him the
mortal wound. The truth was, however, that several gentlemen
voted for McLean on this ballot who would not have given him
their votes had there been the slightest chance for his success.
The genuine McLean vote was about 160. It was known Tuesday night, and I tried to telegraph the fact then, but a storm
on the mountains prevented, that Fremont had a majority of
about twenty over all other candidates. Of course it was vain
to contend against this.[9]

The Nomination of Fremont

The immense hall was crowded in every corner. There was
not a seat anywhere unoccupied, or a space large enough
to stand in that was not filled. The hall was badly ventilated;
the air outside was sultry, and the heat within soon became
terrible. It was enough to knock a man down to draw his
breath. The perspiration poured from every pore of every delegate. Shirt collars drooped "like leaves of the forest when
Autumn hath blown," and fans seemed to be unserviceable, as
the more such air was stirred the hotter it became. The hour
was between six and seven o'clock. An effort had been made to

have Fremont nominated by acclamation, without an informal ballot, as it was palpable that his nomination was inevitable. Colonel Watson Webb favored this idea; so did Honorable David Wilmot, of Pennsylvania. But some of the McLean men objected, and after the disposal of some business, which was "rung in," the convention proceeded to the call of states, and amid the most breathless interest the ballot was taken. It was overwhelmingly Fremont. Then another was made to declare the nomination of Fremont unanimous. The chair put the question thus: "All who are in favor of nominating John C. Fremont as the candidate of this convention for the presidency, will signify the same by giving three cheers!" And three times three perfect Davy Crockett war-whoops, with a touch of the buffalo bull and the wild cat, were given with stunning effect. The scene at the nomination of Buchanan was tame in comparison. A banner evidently prepared for the occasion, was held in readiness on the platform, on which was inscribed, "For President, John C. Fremont." It was spread out and hailed with thunderous plaudits, long continued and wildly emphatic. Nearly all the McLean men acquiesce in the nomination, but there are those among them who growl of the manner in which the Fremont men carried the day by storm, as it were. They wanted more slow, deliberative and conservative action. In short they wanted the ticket to be McLean for President and Fremont for Vice-President, and thought it very strange and hard that such a compromise was not acceptable. They had forgotten that the day of compromises was past, and that the paramount contest now under headway, must be met, in the North, by the young men.

*   *   *

The John McLean men—who were, in general, the antique Whigs—were very sore and disposed to growl last night, and prophesy defeat and all things horrible. This they have a perfect right to do, and it would not seem unreasonable, did they not constantly insist, with the most unctuous eloquence, that with McLean they could have swept the Union. This makes the thing funny. Venerable Whiggery made a stronger effort here to rejuvenate than I would have believed it could have done, had I not observed the operation. But the name of Judge McLean could not save it.

It is not improbable that some degree of surprise and dissatisfaction may be felt out West, at the sudden withdrawal of the name of Salmon P. Chase. The fact is, clearly, that he was withdrawn because there was no apparent possibility of nominating him. The question is—How did this state of facts come to pass? That Chase is the representative man of the movement that should have been made here, is unquestionable. But his especial friends thought this so palpable, and had such confidence in this convention, that they did not work as they might have done. This was one point. But hoary Whiggery was silently but hard at work, and divided the delegation from Ohio, which, in the convention weakened Chase more morally than in votes. The great cause of the want of strength in the convention of Mr. Chase, is, however, to be traced to New York, the politicians of which state have an irresistible desire to do something extraordinary and desperate. It has been plain that Mr. William H. Seward, whom New Yorkers delight to puff as the "foremost man in all this country," as I have heard the phrase here a dozen times, was not the man for the occasion. While opposed to the extension of slavery, he has been in favor of nearly every scheme of public plunder which has come before the Senate since he has been a member thereof. He would not do, and his friends, not being willing to see the leadership of the Republican Party given to a statesman of the West, felicitously took up the idea of a man "fresh from the people," and thinking of free territory, suggested the explorer of that territory, and then, first the politicians of the East, then of the Northwest, saw in John C. Fremont the "coming man". . . .

On the formal ballot, Fremont received all the votes except one Pennsylvania vote for Seward, and twenty-three Pennsylvania votes for McLean, and fourteen Ohio votes for McLean.

The Vice Presidential Nomination

After an informal ballot this morning, in which William L. Dayton, of New Jersey, received the highest vote, a delegate from Massachusetts withdrew, authoritatively and peremptorily, the names of Nathaniel P. Banks, Henry Wilson, and Charles Sumner. Banks had written not to allow his name to be used. Wilson had declined without qualification to allow the use of his name. And Massachusetts could not spare, so her delegates said, Charles Sumner from the floor of the Senate. The pride of that commonwealth in her Senator had not been wounded when he had been prostrated on that floor by a bludgeon. She wanted him still where his voice might be heard. Joseph M. Root, of Ohio, withdrew the name of Tom Ford, who had received several votes, saying that Ford had said some of the boys might want him to run for Vice-President, but he wanted to go into this fight without a knapsack on his back. He could fight best light. Root said that the Buckeye boys wanted Ford for home consumption. The convention then proceeded to a formal ballot. . . .

The nomination of William Dayton, of New Jersey, for the vice presidency by the Republican Party, was a concession to the ultra conservatives, or McLean men.[10] The Fremonters, buoyant in conscious strength, had nominated their man by storm, in spite of all entreaties, prayers, threats, and protestations. The dry bones of the late Whig Party cracked under their rapid, resistless march. Having gained their great point, and having no especial choice for Vice-President, they were willing to use the vice presidential nomination as a poultice on the sore just opened, and conceded that McLean's friends might name the man. The strongest opponent of Mr. Dayton was Colonel Abraham Lincoln of Illinois. It was supposed that Illinois was a doubtful state, and her delegates asked for Lincoln. But there were more apprehensions concerning Jersey than Illinois, and as the Pennsylvanians could not agree upon a man of their state, Jersey named Dayton, and he was at once the man.

During the time that nominations of candidates for the vice presidential candidacy were being made, Colonel William B. Archer, of Illinois, was lauding Colonel Lincoln, of that state, in extravagant terms, and specifying with rather unnecessary particularity many things he (Lincoln) could do, when a delegate inquired, in a loud and solemn tone, "Will he fight?"

Archer is a grey-haired old gent, slightly bent with age, but he jumped straight from the floor, as high as the secretaries' table, and cried out, shrill and wild, "Yes." The audience was convulsed, and a tremendous yell of approbation substantially inserted a fighting plank in the platform. But Archer slightly spoiled the effect of his vaulting performance, adding: "Why, he's from Kentucky, and all Kentuckians will fight." There was a peculiar restlessness and heavy breathing through the multitude, showing that they were strong in the faith that men born north of the Ohio could fight as well as those who had suffered the accident of birth on the other side of that stream. . . .

Dayton, of New Jersey, is thought to be the man. It is said that his record in the Senate is peculiarly *apropos* to the issues now before the people.[11] He is the man who moved the amendment of the Fugitive Slave Law so as to give a trial by jury to fugitives. In New Jersey he is called an Old Fogy, and is known as an Old Line Whig. His nomination is intended to conciliate the McLean men of Pennsylvania and Jersey who are tenderfooted. I think this idea of thus conciliating uncalled for and injudicious, and that the ticket as constituted is not the strongest that could have been manufactured; but we shall see.

Personalities

The amount of enthusiasm, wild excitement, "noise and confusion" in this convention, have been unprecedented. When the name of Charles Sumner was mentioned today, the multitude arose and gave three rousing cheers. A Cincinnati delegate noted for facetiousness, says that it has seemed to him the convention has felt doing that which a fellow was once charged $25 for, viz: "Kicking up a d—— fuss generally."

General J. W. Webb, who has the personal appearance of a very good-looking fine old English gentleman, and is not at all Young Americanish, in making an excited harangue put the question, "Are we wiser than our fathers?" as if there was no possibility of any answer other than a negative one being given, and was startled from his serene poise of self-possession by a very emphatic response from several quarters of "Yes, yes, certainly we are."[12] The audacity of the thing touched the sublime and shows that Young America was certainly about. Webb first smiled, then looked grave and said he did not envy the gentlemen who had so responded, their wisdom or their feelings. . . .

David Wilmot was a candidate during the informal ballot, for Vice-President, but withdrawn by a delegate who was such an enthusiastic admirer of him that he said: "I will name my next boy David Wilmot," whereat the applause was immense. Mr. Wilmot is a gentleman who has attained a fair prospect for immortality at a very cheap rate. The connection of his name with the famous proviso, which he did not draw up, makes him, especially in Republican conventions, a highly distinguished man. He is a short, portly gentleman, his face rotund and rubicund with good living, and wearing an expression of the most obstinate good humor. A smile shines over his broad face whenever he rises to speak. Another of the celebrities present was Robert Emmet, a relative of the illustrious Irishman whose epitaph is yet to be written. He was chosen temporary chairman and made a very pithy, sound and telling speech, the best of the convention.

He is in appearance, unmistakably a cultivated Irishman, and has the "rich brogue" which has attracted so much anti-presidential admiration. It was a significant and cheering sight to see this gentleman engaged in the free state cause. If any poor devils upon the earth have most particular reason to hope that the great territories of the West will become free states, certainly they are the Irish laborers, who are however death on niggers, and have, heretofore, usually given their aid to those who would if they could, make white niggers of Irishmen—those of whom Philemon T. Herbert, of California, the murderer of Thomas Keating, is the best representative.[13] Sitting beside Robert Emmet in the convention, was the world-famous Moses H. Grinnell, the New York merchant prince, who with true princely liberality has patronized the arts and given freely in behalf of science, and lavishly assisted many benevolent enterprises, conspicuous among which is the "Grinnell Expedition" in search of the remains of Sir John Franklin. Mr. Grinnell is a well preserved man of near sixty years of age; the hair on his head is iron grey, and his eyebrows, and whiskers, which he wears in English style, are of the same color, while his face is florid. He was dressed with simple elegance, and showed no disposition to make himself prominent in the convention. His manner of applauding was very enthusiastic, and he frequently so expressed his approbation, thus indicating considerable warmth of temperament. Only once he mounted the platform to make a speech. That was at the critical moment when the names of Chase, Seward, and McLean had been withdrawn, the latter in a manner that caused intense dissatisfaction among his friends, and many of the most ardent of Fremonters were disposed to nominate at once at all hazards.

Thaddeus Stevens, of Pennsylvania, had just warned the convention not to drive away its friends, in substance threatened a bolt, when Grinnell moved a recess, to allow the vehemence of excitement to cool down. He was proceeding to accompany his motion with a few remarks, when the gaunt backwoodsman in the chair, Henry S. Lane, put the question, utterly ignoring the existence of Grinnell, and, in spite of the entreaties of the fine old New York gentleman, declared the house adjourned, though there were many votes against the motion, and Grinnell was gesticulating and calling loudly "one moment, sir! one moment!"

I made one slight mistake in a sketch of the personal appearance of Francis P. Blair.[14] His "badly fitting" teeth are not *artifiical* but *real*. The old fellow's big bald head glistens with intelligence, and he seems to think the result of this convention auspicious. The likeness of Fremont published in the *Tribune* is a perfect caricature, showing only that he wears his hair parted in the middle, which is certainly a strong objection to him. . . .

Faith in Fremont

I wish to give most positive assurances to those who may be inclined to consider this convention a political jest, a thing "full of sound and fury, signifying nothing," that it was very far from being any such thing.[15] The members of the convention had much faith in the power of their cause, and knew that they represented a vast host of intelligent men. They had faith in themselves and faith in their candidate. From the first there was no mistake but Fremont would be the nominee, and there was a very deep and solemn conviction in a large majority of the delegates that he was not only a good man but THE MAN. The faith in him was very remarkable, and was, to me, to a great degree unaccountable. It seemed, and I do not make the comparison irreverently, that a popular instinct, such as sometimes, on great occasions, leaps chasms in logic—for instance, in the case of calling George Washington to be Commander-in-Chief of the American armies of the Revolution—that such an instinct had found in Fremont the man for the times. A feeling of faith in Fremont gathered strength every hour of the sessions of the convention. Every one who knew anything of him said that he was a decisively resolute and honest man, with a fine intellect thoroughly cultivated, and a will that would make him steadfast amid storms. As to the prospect of electing him—Pennsylvania, New Jersey and Illinois were the only free states admitted by the Philadelphia president-makers to be doubtful, and it was held with much confidence that they might be carried. . . .

No More Fusion

There will be no more honest occasion for the Buchanan papers to talk of fusion between the K. N.'s and the Republicans. The Tom Ford affair at New York was an unqualified breakdown. If Edwin D. Morgan, the chairman of the Republican executive committee, had not become frightened before there was the slightest danger of any one being hurt, and made a fool of himself, by opening negotiations with the Apollo Hall Humbug, the Philadelphia convention would have paid no attention whatever to the operations in New York. And as it was, there was an overwhelming majority of the convention in favor of Joshua Giddings' motion to lay the communication from the New York committee on the table; and when Giddings was over-persuaded by Thurlow Weed and others, to move a reconsideration of this motion, the convention merely allowed it to be done, and when David Wilmot reported that no arrangement had been or could be effected with the New York committee, the hall rung with joyful plaudits. There and then the Republican Party parted company with the K. N.'s forever. And foreigners who do not feel willing to be placed on an equality with slave niggers in the free territories, are invited to fall into the ranks, and march to the music of true Democracy. The Spectre of Sam, which has hitherto frightened tens of thousands of honest foreigners from the Republican camp, is at last exorcised—the broad battle field is cleared for action. As for the "isms" of which so much is so foolishly said, Robert Emmet hit the nail on the head and drove it home, by saying —"Let them come with their isms—we'll merge them all into PATRIOTISM!"[16]

Notes

‡   ‡   ‡

INTRODUCTION

[1] Cincinnati *Commercial,* April 29, 1856.

[2] *Three Against Lincoln* (Baton Rouge, 1960), edited by William B. Hesseltine, is a new edition of Murat Halstead's Caucuses of 1860.

[3] Albert Shaw, "Murat Halstead, Journalist," in *Review of Reviews,* 13:439 (April, 1896). "A Great American Journalist," *Review of Reviews,* 38:192 (August, 1908).

[4] Cincinnati *Commercial,* May 29, 1856.

[5] *Ibid.,* April 29, 1856.

[6] *Ibid.,* May 29, 1856.

[7] *Ibid.,* February 18, 1856.

[8] *Ibid.,* February 12, 1856.

[9] "Mr. Fillmore," reported Murat Halstead, "was acting President of the United States. How came he so? By accident. Not a man of the body by which he was selected for the Vice Presidency, thought of him as a President—not a man who voted for him did so with a view to his fitness for the successorship. Who or what he was, few knew and fewer cared. He was a mere consequent. He stopped a hole in the ticket; and, elevated by a casualty, constituted a government as second-hand as his character and official state." Cincinnati *Commercial,* August 28, 1856.

[10] Cincinnati *Commercial,* March 4, 1856.

[11] *Ibid.,* February 26, 1856.

[12] *Ibid.,* February 14, 1856.

[13] *Ibid.,* February 26, 1856.

[14] *Ibid.,* January 5, 1856.

[15] *Ibid.,* May 29, 1856.

[16] *Ibid.,* June 2, 1856.

[17] In October, 1855, Governor Henry A. Wise of Virginia, himself hopeful of the Democratic nomination, concluded to withdraw. "I have never had more than a mere hope of carrying Pennsylvania," he confided to Robert Tyler. "There is too much *Free-soilism* in her to expect a union with the South, except upon a candidate of her own. That was the main cause of my supporting Mr. Buchanan so heartily—it was to bind Pennsylvania to Viriginia." (October 12, 1855). After the nomination, Robert told his father, ex-President John Tyler, "Buchanan . . . is clearly indebted to Virginia for the nomination. Mr. Wise is in truth the Warwick of the hour." (June 13, 1856). Lyon G. Tyler, ed., *Letters and Times of the Tylers* (3 vols., Richmond and Williamsburg, 1884-1896), II, 520, 527. See also Philip G. Auchampaugh, *Robert Tyler, Southern Rights Champion, 1847-1866* (Duluth, 1934), 74-142.

[18] Cincinnati *Commercial,* May 29, 1856.

[19] *Ibid.*

[20] *Ibid.,* June 2, 1856.

[21] *Ibid.,* June 5, 1856.

[22] *Ibid.,* June 9, 1856.

[23] *Ibid.,* June 21, 1856.

[24] *Ibid.,* March 10, 1856.

[25] *Ibid.,* June 10, 1856.

[26] *Ibid.,* July 1, 1856.

[27] *Ibid.,* June 23, 1856.

[28] *Ibid.,* April 29, 1856.

1. FIRST KNOW NOTHING CONVENTION

[1] Cincinnati *Commercial,* February 23, 1856. Telegraphic dispatch.

[2] At the National Council Meeting of the American Party held at Philadelphia in June, 1855, the slavery question nearly disrupted the proceedings. A three-day debate over the twelfth section of the platform ended with a victory for the Southern Know Nothings. The section declared that ". . . Congress possesses no power under the Constitution to legislate upon the subject of slavery in the States . . . or to exclude any State from admission into the Union because her Constitution does or does not recognize the institution of slavery, . . . it is the sense of this National Council that Congress ought not to legislate upon the subject of Slavery within the Territories of the United States. . . ." W. Darrell Overdyke, *The Know-Nothing Party in the South* (Baton Rogue, 1950), 131-133.

John Rufus Edie led delegates from Pennsylvania who had renounced the twelfth section. Their admission over a more conservative delegation from Pennsylvania displeased the Southern members of the National Council. Overdyke, *Know-Nothing Party,* 135.

[3] Cincinnati *Commercial,* February 25, 1856. Telegraphic dispatch.

[4] *Ibid.,* February 26, 1856. Telegraphic dispatch.

[5] *Ibid.,* February 29, 1856.

[6] *Ibid.,* February 25, 1856.

[7] Pap Taylor edited the Cincinnati *Signal,* a rival of the *Commercial.*

[8] Cincinnati *Commercial,* March 4, 1856. Editorials in the *Commercial* frequently bear internal evidence of Halstead's authorship, in whole or in part. Even when they cannot be directly attributed to him they represent his and his associates' opinions on men and events. Fillmore's career is treated in Robert J. Rayback, *Millard Fillmore, Biography of a President* (Buffalo, 1959).

[9] Cincinnati *Commercial,* February 27, 1856.

[10] *Ibid.,* February 29, 1856.

2. REPUBLICAN NATIONAL MASS MEETING

[1] Cincinnati *Commercial,* February 26, 1856.

3. DEMOCRATIC CONVENTION

[1] Cincinnati *Commercial,* April 8, 1856.

[2] *Ibid.,* April 28, 1856.

[3] *Ibid.,* April 30, 1856.

[4] *Ibid.,* May 6, 1856.

[5] A doughface was a Northern politician with Southern principles.

[6] Cincinnati *Commercial,* May 7, 1856.

[7] *Ibid.,* June 3, 1856.

[8] *Ibid.,* May 29, 1856.

[9] *Ibid.,* June 2, 1856.

[10] *Ibid.,* June 3, 1856.

[11] *Ibid.,* June 4, 1856.

[12] Popular, widely advertised line of patent medicines.

[13] Cincinnati *Commercial,* June 4, 1856.

[14] *Ibid.,* June 5, 1856.

[15] At the moment William Walker, soldier of fortune, was at his height in Central America. A native of Tennessee, he had led a filibustering expedition into Nicaragua, and had become dictator of the country. Five weeks after this expression of sympathy by the Democrats, Walker assumed the presidency of Nicaragua. Laurence Greene, *The Filibuster: The Career of William Walker* (Indianapolis, 1937).

[16] Cincinnati *Commercial,* June 5, 1856.

[17] In 1846, President James K. Polk appointed Butler Major-General of volunteers under General Zachary Taylor during the war with Mexico. At Monterey, Butler was second in command. In 1848, Butler won the Democratic party nomination for the vice presidency and ran with Lewis Cass. Butler often wrote poetry and published a book of poems entitled, *The Boatman's Horn and Other Poems.*

[18] In December, 1853, Pierre Soule, then American Minister to Spain, and the Marquis de Turgot, French Ambassador to Spain, duelled over an insulting remark made about Mrs. Soule by Turgot's son-in-law, the Duke of Alba. Soule held Turgot responsible because his son-in-law's remark was made at a party given by Turgot. Soule shot Turgot in the knee. The American Minister formally

expressed regrets to his opponent, but the two failed to achieve a reconciliation. Amos A. Ettinger, *The Mission to Spain of Pierre Soule, 1853-1855* (New Haven, 1932), 226-231.

[19] On June 12, 1854, in a speech at Lafayette, Indiana, Pettit charged Benton with breaking the Missouri Compromise by having an act passed which extended the western boundary of Missouri. Five days later, Benton snarled that Pettit was "a great liar and a dirty dog, falsifying public history for a criminal purpose." *Congressional Globe,* 33 Congress, I session (1854), 1875.

[20] Cincinnati *Commercial,* June 6, 1856.

[21] *Ibid.*, June 7, 1856.

[22] The official report gave slight variations for the totals. cf. *Official Proceedings of the National Democratic Convention Held in Cincinnati, June 2-6, 1856* (Cincinnati, 1856), 66.

[23] Malakhov was a hill overlooking the Crimean city of Sevastopol. During the Crimean War, which Murat Halstead covered as a correspondent, the French captured this fortified hill after a long seige. Its capture sealed the fate of Sevastopol.

[24] Halstead had a low opinion of Breckinridge. "In our mind, we had placed Mr. Breckenridge a degree above this order of bloviating soft-horns. We really supposed him to be something more than 'a promising young Kentucky orator,' and deeply and sincerely do regret to find that we have been mistaken. It is sad to reflect how that laudable ambition to excel in eloquence, for which Kentucky is so indebted to the example of Henry Clay, is defeated in her sons for lack of brains. Nothing but incorrigible shallowness—an absence of common sense equivalent to a vacuum—could have brought John C. Breckinridge to the North side of the Ohio river to tell the people—as he virtually does—that unless he is chosen Vice-President of the United States, with a thick-witted old fellow from Pennsylvania for President—this great Union will be dissolved into jarring sections at war with each other. Nothing but a failure of judgment, such as would seem to have required a positive and very successful effort to be foolish, could have induced him to place himself in a position at once so obnoxious and so untenable." Cincinnati *Commercial,* September 8, 1856.

[25] Cincinnati *Commercial,* June 9, 1856.

[26] *Ibid.*, June 11, 1856.

4. SECOND KNOW NOTHING CONVENTION

[1] Cincinnati *Commercial,* March 10, 1856. Tom Ford was an Ohio Know Nothing politician who was elected Lieutenant Governor in 1855.

[2] Cincinnati *Commercial,* June 16, 1856.

[3] George Law had won fame and fortune as a contractor on canals and railroads. He had entered banking, and owned a line of steamships. In February, 1855, the Pennsylvania legislature endorsed Law for the Know Nothing presidential nomination. His preliminary "campaign biography" asserted that he lacked an essential qualification for the presidency—he had not "served an apprenticeship in doing murders on a battlefield, or doing roguery in a law office."

[4] Cincinnati *Commercial,* June 17, 1856.

[5] Favorite nickname used by members of the American party to confuse the curious. "Sam" was a mysterious individual who was "the embodiment of liberty" and whose creed was the Constitution.

[6] Banks' schemes are fully treated in Fred Harvey Harrington's *Fighting Politician: Major General N. P. Banks* (Philadelphia, 1948).

[7] Cincinnati *Commercial,* June 18, 1856.

[8] The second Know Nothing convention nominated Nathaniel P. Banks for President and William F. Johnston of Pennsylvania for Vice-President. Banks later withdrew in favor of John C. Fremont, the Republican candidate, and after the Republicans refused to support Johnston for the vice presidency, he, too, withdrew.

5. REPUBLICAN CONVENTION

[1] Cincinnati *Commercial,* June 10, 1856.

[2] *Ibid.,* June 9, 1856.

[3] *Ibid.,* April 29, 1856.

[4] *Ibid.,* April 17, 1856.

[5] *Ibid.,* June 18, 1856.

[6] *Ibid.,* June 20, 1856.

[7] *Ibid.,* June 21, 1856.

[8] "This Convention of Delegates, assembled in pursuance of a call addressed to the people of the United States, without regard to past political differences or divisions, who are opposed to the repeal of the Missouri Compromise; to the policy of the present Administration; to the extension of Slavery into Free Territory; in favor of the admission of Kansas as a Free State; of restoring the action of the Federal Government to the principles of Washington and Jefferson; and for the purpose of presenting candidates for the offices of President and Vice-President, do

Resolve: That the maintenance of the principles promulgated in the Declaration of Independence, and embodied in the Federal Constitution, are essential to the preservation of our Republican institutions, and that the Federal Constitution, the rights of the States, and the union of the States, must and shall be preserved.

Resolved: That with our Republican fathers, we hold it to be a self-evident truth, that all men are endowed with the inalienable right to life, liberty, and the pursuit of happiness, and that the primary object and ulterior design of our Federal Government were to secure these rights to all persons under its exclusive jurisdiction; that as our Republican fathers, when they had abolished Slavery in all our National Territory, ordained that no person shall be deprived of life, liberty, or property, without due process of law, it becomes our duty to maintain this provision of the Constitution against all attempts to violate it for the purpose of establishing Slavery in the Territories of the United States by positive legislation, prohibiting its existence or extension therein. That we deny the authority of Congress, of a Territorial Legislature, of any individual, or association of individuals, to give legal existence to Slavery in any Territory of the United States. . . .

Resolved: That the Constitution confers upon Congress sovereign power over the Territories of the United States for their government; and that in the exercise of this power, it is both the right and the imperative duty of Congress to prohibit in the Territories those twin relics of barbarism — Polygamy and Slavery.

Resolved: That while the Constitution of the United States contains ample provisions for the protection of the life, liberty and property of every citizen, the dearest Constitutional rights of the people of Kansas have been fraudulently and violently taken from them;

Their Territory has been invaded by an armed force;

Spurious and pretended legislative, judicial and executive officers have been set over them, by whose usurped authority, sustained by the military power of the government, tyrannical and unconstitutional laws have been enacted and enforced;

The right of the people to keep and bear arms has been infringed;

Test oaths of an extraordinary and entangling nature have been imposed as a condition of exercising the right of suffrage and holding office;

The right of an accused person to a speedy and public trial by an impartial jury has been denied;

The right of the people to be secure in their persons, houses, papers, and effects, against unreasonable searches and seizures, has been violated;

They have been deprived of life, liberty, and property without due process of law;

The freedom of speech and of the press has been abridged;

The right to choose their representatives has been made of no effect;

Murders, robberies, and arsons have been instigated or encouraged, and the offenders have been allowed to go unpunished;

That all these things have been done with the knowledge, sanction, and procurement of the present National Administration; and that for this high crime against the Constitution, the Union, and humanity, we arraign that Administration, the President, his advisers, agents, supporters, apologists, and accessories, either *before* or *after* the fact, before the country and before the world; and that it is our fixed purpose to bring the actual perpetrators of these atrocious outrages and their accomplices to a sure and condign punishment hereafter.

Resolved, That Kansas should be immediately admitted as a State of this Union, with her present Free Constitution, as at once the most effectual way of securing to her citizens the enjoyment of the rights and privileges to which they are entitled, and of ending the civil strife now raging in her territory.

Resolved, That the highwayman's plea, that "might makes right," embodied in the Ostend Circular, was in every respect unworthy of American diplomacy, and would bring shame and dishonor upon any Government or people that gave it their sanction.

Resolved, That a railroad to the Pacific Ocean, by the most central practicable route, is imperatively demanded by the interests of the whole country, and that the Federal Government ought to render immediate and efficient aid in its construction, and as an auxiliary thereto, to the immediate construction of an emigrant road on the line of the railroad.

Resolved, That appropriations by Congress for the improvement of rivers and harbors, of a national character, required for the accommodation and security of an existing commerce, are authorized by the Constitution, and justified by the obligation of Government to protect the lives and property of its citizens.

Resolved, That we invite the affiliation and co-operation of the men of all parties, however differing from us in other respects, in support of the principles herein declared. . . ." *Proceedings of the First Three Republican National Conventions of 1856, 1860 and 1864, Including Proceedings of the . . . Convention Held at Pittsburg /sic/ in February, 1856, as Reported by Horace Greeley* (Minneapolis, 1893), 43-44.

[9] Judge McLean himself was quite disappointed by Spalding's hasty action. Cf. Francis P. Weisenburger, *The Life of John McLean: A Politician on the United States Supreme Court* (Columbus Ohio, 1937) 148 ff.

[10] Cincinnati *Commercial,* June 23, 1856.

[11] *Ibid.,* June 21, 1856.

[12] *Ibid.,* June 23, 1856.

[13] On May 8, 1852, Philip T. Herbert, member of the United States House of Representatives from California, shot and killed Thomas Keating, a waiter, at Willard's hotel in Washington, D. C. Herbert was indicted, but soon acquitted and released.

[14] Cincinnati *Commercial,* June 21, 1856.

[15] *Ibid.,* June 23, 1856.

[16] There was a fifth political convention in 1856. On September 16, delegates from twenty-five states assembled in Baltimore for the last Whig Convention ever to be held. Hundreds of visitors came from nearby Virginia, North Carolina, Maryland, New York, and Pennsylvania. Washington Hunt, who was to preside over the Constitutional Union Party convention in 1860 was temporary chairman, and the permanent president was Edward Bates who, in 1860, would be a candidate for the Republican nomination for the presidency and who was Lincoln's attorney-general. The convention met for two days, listened to speeches deploring the inadequacy of the Pierce administration, deploring the rise of the sectional Republican party, and pledging eternal fealty to the Union and the Constitution. "All who revere the Constitution and the Union," declared the formal resolutions, "must look with alarm at the parties in the field in the present Presidential canvass. . . . The success of either faction must add fuel to the flame which now threatens to wrap our dearest interests in one common ruin." Fortunately, the Convention found one candidate who was bound to neither sectional interest, who was "eminent alike for wisdom and firmness," "justice and moderation," and a "calm, pacific temper"—Millard Fillmore! The party called for a "spontaneous rising of the Whigs throughout the country."

Murat Halstead did not deign to attend this "gathering of a handful of superannuated Whig politicians," and his *Commercial* carried only the bare telegraphic accounts of the meeting. In the editors' opinion, "these gentlemen are evidently incapable of the idea that the process now going on in the politics of the United States is a *Revolution*" and they would be swept away by the new forces loosened upon the country. "It is difficult to say whether this poor attempt to disinter and galvanize dead Whiggery is more ludicrous or melancholy." Cincinnati *Commercial,* September 17, 18, 19, and 22, 1856.

Index

† † †

*   *   *